Praise for *Software Ou*

MW00355794

"There are many shifts occurring today as companies implement their digital business strategies. One aspect of this shift—companies are adjusting their approach to outsourcing in part by reinsourcing systems critical to their new technology-driven strategies. The problem is that there is little research or information available on transferring application systems knowledge and ownership from one organization to another—until now. In *Software Ownership Transfer,* Vinod draws on his experiences, large and small, in making such critical transfers. I particularly like his distinction between knowledge transfer and ownership—not ownership in the legal sense, but ownership in the sense of a team taking 'ownership' of their new responsibility. Knowledge transfer is only the first step in ownership transfer. If you are contemplating the transfer of an application system—from a vendor to in-house or from one internal location to another (as happens often today)—then you need to use this book as a model for making your transfer a success."

—*Jim Highsmith, author of* Agile Project Management,
coauthor of The Agile Manifesto

"Software is becoming increasingly central to most modern organizations. Indeed, it has become trite to observe that one should no longer have a 'digital strategy' or a 'technology strategy': These strategies now form the core of the business strategy itself. This shift is seeing many organizations reconsider their software-sourcing strategy, such as, for example, bringing back in-house resources that they previously outsourced. The process of transferring the 'ownership' of core digital products is complex and can frequently be the source of disappointment, to say the least. In the worst case, significant investments can be lost in the transfer process. In this book, Vinod Sankaranarayanan draws upon his significant experience in digital product ownership and transfer, backed by copious real-life examples, and draws some important recommendations for any leader or organization overseeing a transition between teams, whether internal or external. A highly recommended read for any leader who is contemplating or is in the process of a digital product transfer."

—*Chris Murphy, group managing director, Europe,*
Middle East, and South Asia, ThoughtWorks

"Vinod has written a compelling book on a topic that is generating a lot of interest today but whose business outcomes are not yet clear. Combining his own rich experience as a practitioner of Agile techniques with a lucid narrative style, Vinod provides many insightful perspectives to address the challenging yet essential function of ownership transfer of IT projects. More importantly, Vinod has been able to bring structure and practical application to an area that most often than not is ad-hoc and ambiguous. This piece of work is an important step in addressing a question that will become more and more relevant in the complex world of IT outsourcing and offshoring in the years to come."

—*Rizwan Hazarika, CIO and cloud advisory services lead,*
ASEAN region, IBM

"Knowledge transfer is an area that too many executives are willing to throw under the bus (along with QA) when budgets and deadline pressures begin to loom. Vinod provides a compelling rationale for understanding why knowledge transfer needs to be planned as a normal part of the SDLC. We ignore his analysis at our own peril!"

—*John Peebles, senior vice-president,*
digital media at Sothebys

"Every once in a while, the care and feeding of software assets changes hands in enterprise IT. This may be because of a decision to outsource, insource, or simply switch vendors. The quality of the handover is crucial, as Vinod points out in this one-of-a-kind book. But handovers receive less attention than required—in practice as well as in theory—as evidenced by the lack of books on this topic. Handovers are typically dealt with as a three-month transition exercise, usually irrespective of the size and complexity of the transition. Post-transition performance almost always dips as a result, and it takes years to recover. *Software Ownership Transfer* provides excellent insights on what it takes to avoid post-transition blues."

—*Sriram Narayan, author of* Agile IT
Organization Design *and IT management*
consultant at ThoughtWorks

"Typically in a project-transition context, the environment is hostile as one team is losing the work and the other is taking it over, which leads to not-so-productive outcomes. Vinod has brought in a new approach to the situation, using Agile principles and values, making it a more collaborative effort. The book is a good read with rich elucidation of experiences and case studies of real-life engagements."

—*Vishwesher Hegde, partner, PM Power Consulting*

"Every organization has to deal with ownership changes in software projects. Hardly any organization, however, consciously plans for such transitions to be successful. The costs of poorly executed ownership transfers are huge and have a permanent impact on the organization and its business. Vinod Sankaranarayanan, in this book, draws upon his extensive experience in the software industry to build a framework and a step-by-step guide for us to use whenever we execute ownership transfers in our teams, organizations, or business-units. This book is a must-read and a must-have for IT project leaders and architects.

It is guaranteed to increase the chances of software ownership transfer success manifold."

—*Vishy Ranganath, director of product development at Intuit*

"I would suggest this book for anyone transferring any IT service. No matter how many transfers you have been a part of (specific service, acquisition, divestiture, etc.), there's always a gotcha you need to look out for, and this book makes you aware of most of them. Personally, I found the areas of Agile consideration to be most beneficial because this is so relevant for today's mature development organizations. It's obvious Vinod took his time to make this book so clear even the most non-techy of techies can understand it. It's easy to understand if you are a developer, manager, PM, or exec."

—*Armando Morales, senior manager, Cisco IT*

"Knowledge transition is one of the most important phases of a software development lifecycle. Vinod has very beautifully captured various aspects of the process and has given great suggestions so that other projects could benefit from it. The book has an interesting narrative based on real-life experiences and practical situations that keeps the reader engaged. While the book would be useful for any software development methodology, the Agile way of doing the knowledge transition makes sure that both the parties actively pair during the transition to ensure the ownership transfer and not just to complete yet another milestone."

—Pravin Thakur, offshore development head, Thetrainline.com

"This book is a good reference for the ownership-transfer approach. It covers aspects related to both management and engineering practices. Vinod has very well explained his experience, to which we can relate."

—Anish Cheriyan, director-quality, Huawei Technologies, India

"Ownership transfer is not an everyday affair in project delivery. Neither is it so rare that people in the industry can wish it away. It is a crucial phase of projects and lays the foundation for a new beginning. At the same time, it is a perilous path as this phase brings with it many unknown unknowns. It is also dangerous because leaders are not always in control of situations given the multi-party involvement. Vinod brings out much needed attention and focus to an underrated topic through this book. The book provides details on both hard and soft aspects that play out during an ownership transfer. It also brings an interesting angle on using Agile principles for such activities. A must read for technologists who want to handle such transitions professionally."

—Padmanabhan Kalyanasundaram, head of the delivery excellence group at Mindtree

"We are starting to see the influence of Agile combined with digitization in almost every organization. Ownership of these initiatives is a key criterion to making Agile successful in today's fast-paced tech world. Vinod has captured the essence of ownership in delightful detail, including the challenges and pitfalls, which are illustrated very well with real-life examples. He brings in a refreshing approach to taking ownership utilizing the fundamental principles of Agile. A very useful book for transition managers and all members in the delivery organization."

—Jijo Olassa, CEO and cofounder, Verbat Technologies

"Project transitions are common in a multi-actor world. One of the key components of transition is knowledge transfer. Vinod provides a practitioner's multidimensional perspective on best practices to adopt covering technical and human-related aspects. It covers Lean Agile, the three bridges, and specific measurement metrics to quantify the efficacy of the process. These are based on real-life experiences from the trenches. If you are interested in quickly executing the insights in this book, you would find the Things to Know and Do sections extremely crisp and actionable. Overall it fills a much needed knowledge gap and can serve as an execution playbook for effective project transfers."

—*Derick Jose, cofounder, Flutura*

"Vinod has put together a compelling book that illustrates how *not* to be doing knowledge transfers. He has then married Agile philosophies to provide a completely different take on knowledge transfers, or *ownership transfers*, as he calls them. Since I had run a similar exercise, I could relate to a lot of the principles in the book. Coming from a product management background, I was particularly interested in the concept of 'continuous business'. The narrative-driven style ensures that the book is an easy read. The approaches given in this book will aid any IT organization as they execute their restructuring efforts or revamp their sourcing strategies."

—*Linda Taylor, product manager,*
thetrainline.com

"This book addresses a topic missing in current literature. It provides a valuable addition to the professional literature. In particular, the text is based upon the actual experiences of the author and his team. Numerous real-life examples are cited and bring the text a rich sense of practical advice. More important, the author has generalized the team experience and shown how this knowledge may be applied generally. While the book focuses primarily upon the issues faced by teams who use an Agile approach, most of the topics can be applied more globally. I have participated in ownership transfer, especially in the re-insourcing of IT services from Electronic Data Systems to the Blue Shield of California client team. Almost all of that development had been accomplished in a more traditional fashion. We would have benefited greatly from having a guidebook such as this to assist us."

—*Daniel Scott, chief consultant,*
LD Scott Consulting

"A thorough and interesting account of a complex handover. This book talks candidly about a topic that the industry prefers not to address openly. This unique insight provides lessons for anyone thinking about taking over or handing over the development and running of a system. Seeing where others have succeeded and failed gives real practical guidance on everything from the structuring of contracts to the running of the teams."

—*Brett Ansley, CPO, VictoriaPlum.com*

"Organizations constantly strive for operational excellence, which also translates into expensive initiatives in the form of business transformation projects. The most crucial aspect of these projects is not about going for the best solution but about ensuring transition into superior business processes with minimal disruption. Every servicing organization has a certain well-documented methodology for these transition activities. However, most of these methodologies suffer from near-sighted or one-sided risk mitigation strategies (for the vendor only) and often result in frustration and unhappiness on the client's part. Vinod is putting together a well-defined framework around this critical aspect of project delivery. This book will be a handy tool for novices as well as for seasoned professionals in providing a structured framework for transition with crucial business transformation projects. The emphasis on Agile methodology for knowledge transfer is very relevant right now as more and more customers are moving out of waterfall delivery expectations and are aiming for quicker payback from their investments. This book will help servicing vendors in delivering critical projects smoothly sans any operational risk or any cultural shock alike."

—*Gaurav Mishra, enterprise data architect,*
BMO Harris Bank

"Knowledge transition is important to any project. Vinod has shown how it can be made collaborative and effective while focusing on business continuity with his vast experience in ownership transfers. This book is useful for anyone attempting to move projects between teams located anywhere."

—*Pramod Sadalage, coauthor of* NoSQL
Distilled *and* Refactoring Databases:
Evolutionary Database Design

"Each IT application transfer project has its nuances and while there is a framework and best-practice guideline—the success or otherwise of a project is based on a clear understanding of its nuances and challenges, which would then pave the way for a well thought-out transfer program. Vinod has articulated well the need to strike a balance between leveraging such a standard framework and chalking out a fit-for-purpose program. Vinod has further brought this out through some options, such as, for instance, by outlining the efficacy of DevOps model, a model that seems to stand a much better chance of succeeding. IT application transfer projects often go off rails due to a short-term focus. Vinod has again described the importance of defining a scope that looks beyond the short-term milestones and considers the overall needs of the business—that is, the sustainability of the outcome of such transfer projects. A critical success factor for an IT application transfer project is the need for upfront and continuing trust among all stakeholders, and more importantly, an alignment on the mutual benefit of the project. Vinod has articulated well the people dynamics and how an 'upfront foundation of trust' could cut out wastes in the process and ensure that teams are working for a common purpose. Blatantly obvious, but Vinod has stressed the importance of this dynamic in a very compelling manner."

—*Ravikumar MR, head of strategic*
operations- global markets,
Allied World Assurance Company

"This book is not a theoretical dissertation on transferring ownership of a software project; it is a usable reference guide on how to set up a project to enable successful transition. Many of the ideas generated will lead to a healthy team environment and make for better all-around product delivery."

—*Sameer Deans, delivery partner*
(principal consultant)

"This book is an excellent treatise on a highly critical subject, which is often not only taken for granted but also done incorrectly. The book is even more credible as Vinod has expounded the topic based on his extensive practical experience. IT products and solutions are highly valuable knowledge-based assets, and therefore it is imperative that the 'ownership' of knowledge transfer be done diligently. The approach propounded by Vinod, which is based on Agile principles, will certainly help in significantly reducing the disruptions and uncertainties not only during the transfer process, but more importantly, after the transfer as well."

—*Sunil Mundra, Agile principal consultant,*
ThoughtWorks

"In a fast-paced world where knowledge transfer is often outstripped by the speed of business—with the next project often takes focus before the last project is fully embedded and sustainably maintained—Vinod provides much-needed practical insights that bring agility to this last mile of implementation."

—*Betty Enyonam Kumahor, managing partner,*
The Cobalt Partners

"This book breaks the misconception that software ownership transfer is confined to knowledge transfer. Through various anecdotes, Vinod takes us on a journey of the complete spectrum of software ownership transfer, discussing the technology issues, process issues, people issues, emotional issues, security issues, stakeholder expectations, etc. He also gives practical information on how to use Agile methodology in ownership transfer and how we measure progress. A good read if you are involved in any kind of software ownership transfer."

—*Dattatri Salagame, COO – digital transformation and*
enterprise solutions, Happiest Minds Technologies

"In an IT application knowledge-transition scenario, it is the ownership transfer that makes or breaks the day. This is seldom understood. Vinod has brought out this aspect with good anecdotes from other situations as well."

—*Ramesh Ramakrishnan,*
Tata Consultancy Services

"The book provides some excellent examples and food for thought to anyone who is considering or about to embark on the perilous journey that is software ownership transfer. Pulling from the concepts and principals of Agile development, as well as from the author's own broad experience, the reader will be well armed with a list of considerations to help them work through the handover process. A worthwhile read!"

—*Cecile Diener, product manager, Equidelta*

Software Ownership Transfer

Software Ownership Transfer

Evolving Knowledge Transfer for the Agile World

Vinod Sankaranarayanan

✦✦ Addison-Wesley

Boston • Columbus • Indianapolis • New York • San Francisco
Amsterdam • Cape Town • Dubai • London • Madrid • Milan • Munich
Paris • Montreal • Toronto • Delhi • Mexico City • São Paulo • Sidney
Hong Kong • Seoul • Singapore • Taipei • Tokyo

Library of Congress Control Number: 2016942744

ISBN-13: 978-0-13-418101-1
ISBN-10: 0-13-418101-8

Text printed in the United States on recycled paper at RR Donnelley in Crawfordsville, Indiana.

1   16

Editor-in-Chief
Mark Taub

Acquisitions Editor
Chris Guzikowski

Managing Editor
Sandra Schroeder

Senior Project Editor
Lori Lyons

Production Manager
Ellora Sengupta

Copy Editor
Linda Morris

Indexer
Erika Millen

Proofreader
Jaikumar

Technical Reviewer
Sriram Narayan
Ramesh Ramakrishnan
Pramodkumar Sadalage
Pravin Kumar Thakur
Anish Cheriyan

Editorial Assistant
Olivia Basegio

Cover Designer
Chuti Prasertsith

Compositor
codeMantra

To my wife Vidya. She endures everything and endears everyone.

Contents

Register your copy of *Software Ownership Transfer* at informit.com for convenient access to downloads, updates, and corrections as they become available. To start the registration process, go to informit.com/register and log in or create an account. Enter the product ISBN 9780134181011 and click Submit. After the process is complete, you will find any available bonus content under "Registered Products."

Figure List

Preface

In 1990, C. K. Prahalad and Gary Hamel argued for organizations to focus on their core competence.[1] In many ways, this planted the seed for large enterprises to outsource their IT activities. It was around this time that IT service organizations bloomed and mushroomed. Many IT activities were first outsourced, then offshored. Organizations derived cost arbitrage, a 24-7 work cycle, apart from de-risking their information and knowledge assets.[2] The geographic spread of outsourcing provides business continuity guarantee. Twenty-five years later, almost every Fortune 500 company has either executed outsourcing and offshoring or, at a minimum, given considerable thought to its outsourcing strategies.

But times have changed. Today's world is replete with the paradigms of the Lean methodology, innovation, disruption, and of course, Agile. Indeed, we are witnessing another wave of Schumpeterian creative destruction.[3] Younger companies are leapfrogging established players to create products that are far more sophisticated and personalized. These changes are forcing organizations to rethink their sourcing strategies. Offshoring has given way to near-shoring (relocating to locations in neighboring countries), on-shoring (relocating to low-cost destinations within the same country), and, of course, insourcing (taking work back into the organization).[4]

At an organizational level, these sourcing strategies translate into ownership changes for application platforms. Applications and projects change hands as portfolios get realigned among the members of management. In this book, the focus is to explore how these ownership transfers can be executed with minimum risk and maximum efficiency. Ownership transfers are a consequence of organizational restructuring. Organizational restructuring is a vast subject in itself and perhaps requires another book. Hence, I have not dealt here on why these transfers occur.

As I wrote this book, the title underwent several changes. I started with *Agile Knowledge Transfer*. My then MD (managing director) at ThoughtWorks, Sunder Malyandi, suggested that this should be positioned at the decision-maker's level. Agile is serving a larger purpose, and that larger purpose is transferring ownership. I then changed the name to *Ownership Transfer,* but this title seemed confusing to many

---

1. https://hbr.org/1990/05/the-core-competence-of-the-corporation
2. https://www.flatworldsolutions.com/articles/top-ten-reasons-to-outsource.php
3. https://en.wikipedia.org/wiki/Creative_destruction
4. http://www.mckinsey.com/insights/business_technology/rebalancing_your_sourcing_strategy

people. It did not seem like an IT topic. After discussions with my editor and some of the book's reviewers, I then adopted *Software Ownership Transfer* as the title.

This is a perceptive book. I have drawn heavily on my experience in the IT industry to write this book. The literature in this space is quite sparse. Therefore, I have relied on interviews and focus group discussions with industry veterans to validate my hypotheses and fine-tune my suggestions.

During my interviews, it became apparent that what worked in my experience might not work for everyone else, at least right away. Although all of the interviewees agreed with the suggestions in the book, they felt constrained to practice them within their organization. Differences within management practices, business cultures, and sales organizations (in the case of IT service organizations) were all cited as impediments to adopt these measures. Interestingly, these are some of the same challenges in adopting the Agile methodology as well. Many interviewees told me that ownership transfers in their paradigm was a mix of development, maintenance, and operations. This industry witnesses large outsourcing deals running into hundreds of millions of dollars over several years.

The ideas suggested in this book may work well for Agile organizations, but they might be difficult to adopt within organizations that have deep divisions amongst development, maintenance, and operations streams. The ideas presented are more likely to work well in outcome-oriented teams as opposed to activity-oriented teams.[5] They may work well for teams that take a product view and teams that adopt a model in which development and operations work very closely with each other.

This is not meant to be an introductory book. This book assumes that the reader has experience in software delivery, appreciates Agile, and understands Lean methodology and Continuous Delivery. This book does not address every question about the transition process, nor is it meant for transitions in which the predominant focus is to rebadge incumbent team members to a new organization. Addressing all these topics would be like trying to boil the ocean. At the same time, there are some situations in the book that even a reader from the operations world can relate to. The book is not meant to be an exhaustive checklist of what to do in an ownership transfer, but rather one that analyzes many of the problems involved in ownership transfer.

The reader is urged to draw lessons from the many experiences and insights drawn in the chapters. I have discussed this topic in several forums and the most common concern of every practitioner is to keep morale high during the transition. It is the biggest challenge when undertaking this type of an exercise. It is the elephant in the room. However, keeping a team motivated is a leadership issue. The way each person solves this problem is a function of their personality, the culture within that group,

---

5. Sriram Narayan, Agile IT Organization Design http://www.agileorgdesign.com/p/table-of-contents-preface.html

and the policies in effect in that organization. Having said that, some of the stories in the book provide examples of ways team morale can be maintained.

I believe this subject has not been studied enough, and even with this book, we have barely gotten our feet wet. I fervently hope that organizations and groups will think beyond a ninety-day templated model for knowledge transfers. I will consider my purpose accomplished if organizations begin to look at ownership transfers holistically and plan for transitions over larger time spans with a deeper appreciation of the scope involved. I would be happy to hear any stories of organizations that realized their mistakes midway through a transfer and were successfully able to correct their course.

Who Can Make These Ideas Work?

This book is meant for medium-to-large organizations (from fifty to several thousand employees) who have significant investment in hardware, software, and personnel. Organizations and ISVs who find a need to execute sourcing transitions differently will find value from this book. IT service providers can use this book to engage effectively with their customers. Investors and business leaders may appreciate the insight that the cost of an ownership transfer is not limited to the cost of the effort expended in the actual transition. When a transition occurs, businesses risk a variety of costs, from the opportunity costs of failing to work on a business-critical project during the transition to the costs of service disruptions after the transfer occurs. This book offers ideas on mitigating these risks. In particular, the type of people who may benefit from some of the suggestions in this book are:

- Senior executives in IT organizations who decide on re-structuring and sourcing strategies
- Senior managers who are entrusted to drive organizational strategies
- Senior management at ISVs
- Executives in charge of procurement and vendor management
- Business heads who interface with IT groups
- Director or VP heading software delivery, product management, and engineering
- Senior Management of IT service providers
- Members of IT governance groups

- Process quality consultants, coaches, and SEPG group members
- Investors and board members deciding on diversification and consolidation strategies

Experience tells me that IT service providers have come to adopt Agile because their customers asked them to. The same will be required with ownership transfer. The ideas from this book have higher chances of success if they are driven from the customer organization. Throughout the book, I have provided many example scenarios and story narratives to make the concepts relatable and personal. Many of these examples are inspired by real-world incidents, but I have used fictitious names for companies and client personnel, and dramatized some incidents. I have retained ThoughtWorks's name because many of my experiences emerge out of my tenure at ThoughtWorks. At the same time, I have taken creative liberties with the incidents in order to better convey the message. Any resemblance to real-life situations is coincidental and unintentional.

These examples are not complete stories in that they do not provide a resolution to the problems; rather, they provide ways to deal with the problem at hand. In every instance where I have seen these approaches succeed, the implementers and their organizations were deeply invested. Their passionate belief and commitment to the cause (often more through deeds than words) ensured that the incumbents and the new members established working relationships and, as a group, became open to experiment and collaborate.

In a similar vein, I do not focus only on success stories. All change involves hard and soft aspects. Like an iceberg, the hard aspects are visible, but they comprise perhaps only ten percent of the efforts involved. The soft aspects are much larger and hidden beneath the surface. The undercurrents beneath the surface are what propels the iceberg forward. These soft aspects demand considerable leadership involvement. One of my aims has been to highlight challenges in running ownership transfers. I believe I have been quite candid in articulating a lot of our mistakes in running these programs. As they say, success inspires, but failure teaches. I am positive that many of the examples illustrated will resonate with your own experiences and the insights presented will aid you in solving future problems.

How to Read This Book

The classic struggle of most authors of this genre is to keep the reader engaged while at the same time pass on knowledge. Hence I chose the narrative format. Throughout this book I used the ownership transfer that occurred at EuroT as a preeminent storyline to discuss various themes on the subject. Chapters 1 and 4 lay out the basis of the EuroT project. Chapters 5 through 12 pick out specific dimensions of this topic and discuss various nuggets of thought.

At the same time, I also included several other stories, such as that of Arival systems, which provide a very different perspective—that of someone taking over an application. Chapters 12 through 15 step away from the storyline to discuss general guidelines on approaches to sizing, measurement, and addressing the complexities arising out of these exercises.

I urge the reader to go over each chapter in the order laid out. For the hurried reader, I have listed a summary section of "Things to Know and Do" at the end of each chapter. For those looking for a lay of the land, I have included the following mind-map. The mind map shown in Figure 0.1 provides a holistic view of all the dimensions covered around ownership transfer. Each of the level 1 subnodes broadly translates into a chapter within the book.

Figure 0.1 *Ownership transfer—mind map*

Register your copy of *Software Ownership Transfer* at informit.com for convenient access to downloads, updates, and corrections as they become available. To start the registration process, go to informit.com/register and log in or create an account. Enter the product ISBN 9780134181011 and click Submit. After the process is complete, you will find any available bonus content under "Registered Products."

Acknowledgments

This book would not have come to life if not for the constant source of motivation from Pravin Thakur, the offshore head for thetrainline.com. He has seen this book evolve from a presentation to a rough script to a complete manuscript. In each stage, he was present to provide his ideas, feedback, and guidance.

David Jack, Group CIO MetaPack, germinated the idea of looking at this discipline as a best practice. That conversation was the seed that goaded me to delve deeper into the world of knowledge transfers.

Pramod Sadalage, renowned database expert and author of many books, put me in touch with Bernard Goodwin at Addison-Wesley, who became my editor until his retirement at the end of 2014. Christopher Guzikowski took over from there and brought my book to its conclusion.

My development editor Michelle Housley had been my constant point of contact starting with the contracting process with Pearson, through the proposal reviews, peer reviews and finally providing me with her valuable development edit insights.

This book has achieved its final form thanks to the copy editing and compilation efforts of Ellora Sengupta and Linda Morris. Their eye for detail continues to amaze me.

I need to thank every friend of mine who readily agreed to participate in our focus group discussions. Those discussions helped validate my hypothesis and suggestions on this topic. Many of you readily shared your personal experiences as well. Some of those have found their way into this book. Thank you Sudheer, Sreeja, Rahul, Sriram, Preethi, and Sudeep.

My reviewers played a critical role in chiseling the theme and structure it to its current form. Their input gave me the opportunity to add several chapters to the book as well. Many thanks to Pramod Sadalage, Babuji Abraham, Ramesh Ramakrishnan, Sriram Narayan, Anish Cheriyan, Vishewshwar Hegde, Sriram Narayanan, Vishy Ranganath, and Ramesh Dorairaj. And of course, many thanks to all those who read over the manuscript and provided endorsements.

I extend my gratitude to the ThoughtWorks operations team, who approved my vacations to work on the manuscript. I also thank Suresh Kalarikkal, who provided legal advice on various aspects on the book.

Ashay Saxena provided access to the Indian Institute of Management, Bangalore (IIMB) campus. The relaxed environs of the sprawling campus blew away my writer's blocks.

I must thank Suchita, Nikhita, and Akshay for sharing their personal experiences with transitions. Their stories have helped me enrich the manuscript.

And finally, my wonderful wife Vidya, who has happily accommodated my cooped-up existence weekend after weekend over several months. And our two handfuls of joy, Dhruv and Dyuthi; our rays of sunshine. They make every dull day a delight.

About the Author

Vinod Sankaranarayanan, a Project Management Consultant at ThoughtWorks, has advised many organizations in the Finance, Travel, Retail, and Healthcare space. Along the way he has handled several large project delivery responsibilities. He has witnessed and driven several sourcing transitions for his clients.

Vinod started his professional career in the pre-Agile era and later adapted to the Agile model of working. This has enabled him to empathize with and provide practical suggestions to clients who often find themselves making Agile transitions and sourcing transitions at the same time.

Vinod has essayed the roles of a business analyst, tester, pre-sales consultant, program manager, account manager, Agile coach, and practice leader as part of his long IT Journey.

Before ThoughtWorks, Vinod worked at Mindtree, a well-known IT services organization. At Mindtree he was one of the founding members of the Business Analysts Council and the Agile Council, focusing on creating organizational capacity to win and execute consulting as well as Agile projects.

He lives in Bangalore with his wife Vidya and their children Dhruv and Dyuthi. An occasional blogger and speaker at conferences, his writings, talks, and contact information are available at ownershiptransfer.in

Introduction

In December 2012, Mason, our development director, flew down to Bangalore. Every time he visited Bangalore, we always kicked off with a Leadership Team meeting. This time, though, Mason had a unique agenda. After having worked together for over five years, the time had come for us to transfer responsibility over to the EuroT team at the headquarters in London. We needed to put a plan in place to transfer work that we traditionally did out of Bangalore over to London. There were many ramifications to this transfer: London needed to pick up more responsibility. Its team size would grow. The team in Bangalore would ramp down. We were not clear if we would have a team in Bangalore any longer or not. We were not sure what and how much could be transferred. We had certainly not assessed the team's reaction to this new course. Not many in London knew of the decision. We essentially needed to chart a course for our ship, but the destination was unclear.

EuroT started off as a travel agency in the late 1980s. It is now a large online travel company specializing in selling bus and train tickets for a huge commuter base in Europe. EuroT's specialty is to bring together schedules and connections from disparate bus and train services across Europe. After the advent of the Internet, EuroT employees realized that travel booking would change forever. In the late 1990s, EuroT was one of the first companies to set up an online reservation system. Since then, they expanded to include payments, personalization, and a slew of other features in their application. Today, they are the preeminent online travel company in Europe. Their website and mobile applications are some of the most popular in Europe. Thousands of commuters use their applications for their daily commutes. More than 20,000 tickets are sold every day on EuroT. The platform witnesses more than eight billion euros in ticket sales every year. EuroT's technology platform is so robust that many other bus and train companies use its engine to power their own ecommerce websites. Thus, EuroT caters both to the business segment and to the consumer market.

ThoughtWorks is a well-known name in the world of Agile software development. They apply avant-garde methods to designing, creating, and delivering software. Spread over 30 offices in 12 countries, their more than 3,500 consultants help organizations large and small to deliver business-enabling software. EuroT had requested that ThoughtWorks review their software design and code.

This relationship, which started as a one-off task, eventually translated into one of the longest and strongest partnerships both organizations ever had, one which ran for many years. As the software platform matured and the business gained robustness and growth, it was time to level down the engagement. Although many factors were behind the decision, the primary driver was EuroT's need to reduce capital expenditure.

That week in 2012 was a busy week for the EuroT Leadership Team. We had trouble figuring out where to start. It seemed a bit like jumbled tape. If you can't get hold of one end, you cannot begin to straighten it out. Systems have a way of becoming complicated. We had created many processes over the five years of partnership—inceptions, releases, defect triages, and nonfunctional testing (or NFT, as we called it). Each stakeholder had a different view on what was crucial. For the development manager, story development was preeminent. The release manager considered defect triage and the release checklist critical. For the test manager, regression and nonfunctional testing were important. Delivery metrics were crucial to the delivery manager.

Some of us realized our current roles may no longer be relevant after the transfer. Discussing such a transformation objectively, especially when you realize that the outcome may make your role redundant, calls for tremendous maturity.

This was a pivotal point for the account. We clearly had to bring everyone up to speed with the direction being taken. We also needed to ensure that the usual way of thinking changed. Decisions on projects, modules, components, and even "business as usual" activities needed to be made with the transfer in mind. Everyone needed to ask additional questions when making decisions. What does it mean for the transfer? Will the Bangalore team be doing this the next time? If not, does someone in London know what needs to be done?

Jason Gots, editor at BigThink, says that there were five big moments in the history of knowledge transfer.[1] The first milestone was when we began using smoke signals. The ancient Chinese used them to communicate military tactics. The Roman College of Cardinals uses the smoke signal to convey the election of a new Pope, even to this day.

The carrier pigeon has a checkered history dating back to Ancient Rome. Their reliability prompted the Pigeon Post of the Great Barrier Island in 1897, a postal service that relied on the pigeons flying across islands to deliver messages. They were used heavily during World Wars I and II.

The printing press allowed further widespread distribution and retention of knowledge. During the Renaissance, printing costs decreased, which allowed for an increase in publishing and sharing knowledge. Although television and radio

---

1. http://bigthink.com/think-tank/5-big-moments-in-the-history-of-knowledge-transfer

are far more dynamic media, they do not store information like printed materials. The printed word allows you to retain information and revisit it as need be.

The telegraph was another watershed event in the era of communication. It allowed simultaneity across the world.

However, all of the previous mediums supported communication that is one step removed. Many of them did not enable synchronous communication, allowing for simultaneity on either side. The Internet has helped break barriers and build bridges. It combines the benefits of all the previous inventions and provides a truly empowered medium for sharing knowledge. Whether through social networks, online classroom sessions, or textual databases, the compendium of information harnessed over the Internet is overwhelming. Although communicating online can never replace being there to share a moment, it can do the next best thing in most cases. Open a champagne bottle on both sides, raise a toast, and clink the LED.

Over the next few chapters, I discuss what I learned over the ensuing months not just from my experience with EuroT, but also from others' experience in similar exercises in other organizations as well. The chapters cover eight major themes: executing ownership transfer, being Agile, ownership, engineering, process, infrastructure, culture, and continuous business. The last chapters are dedicated to how to apply this knowledge to future transfers.

Chapter 1

The Challenge with Knowledge Transfers

Every IT product goes through a knowledge transfer (KT) phase at some point in its lifetime. Quite often it is immediately after development is completed and maintenance has taken over. Sometimes other reasons can trigger a knowledge transition. Outsourcing, an incumbent's poor performance, or business landscape changes can trigger a need to hand over an IT product.

While going through this phase, enterprises often do not have a predictable way of transitioning. In outsourcing scenarios, one relies on the expertise provided by the vendor taking over the application. In cases of restructuring or insourcing, organizations might not have a ready reckoner to look at how these transitions can be handled.

Most IT service organizations use a readymade template for knowledge transfers. The processes in these templates rely on a set methodology of analysis, shadowing, reverse shadowing, and steady state. Some organizations also talk about a stabilization phase. Contracts are signed up with timelines of three months, often followed by a stabilization phase. However, the delivery teams may face inordinate challenges:

- **Challenge 1:** The most obvious challenge is that there is a lot to do within a short span of time. Apart from everything else, assembling the team, knowing the lay of the land, and putting a plan in place will shave off a few weeks from the schedule.

- **Challenge 2:** The next challenge is to get the customer and incumbent to agree to the plan. This may take longer than you expect. In fact, it can take a month or more for people from three different organizations to even get into a working rhythm. It takes time for momentum to build up.

- **Challenge 3:** People soon realize they are falling behind schedule. With strict timelines, there is a tendency to cut corners, and quality begins to suffer.
- **Challenge 4:** Most well-laid plans bring out unknowns. Strict timelines often do not allow for time to unearth the unknowns.

A tactical challenge faced by the new team is getting all the right access to all systems within this timeframe. Assembling members is a crucial step before getting the access rights. Only when the members are assembled can we tell which individual needs what access. After that, we need to identify all of the ports, firewalls, and authorizations required to execute each member's work.

To say that we need to list all the necessary ports, firewalls, and authorizations in one place and then get IS resources to implement the access rights makes things sound simple. The process is rarely that straightforward. In reality, even members who have worked in the group for a long time might not know all the systems to which they require access.

In one of my recent engagements, in which I was working from the client's location, we needed to obtain certain access rights and a hard token to allow members to work remotely. The client manager put us in touch with an old vendor who had remote access. This member had obtained access more than two years back. He came by to help and soon realized that the customer processes had changed. We had to get four different tickets created for different levels of approval, and each ticket required approval from different people. In addition, the tickets expired if approval did not come within two days. It took two to three months for some team members to obtain this access. In another organization, the process of granting administrator privileges on developer work stations had its own unique workflow, and in one extreme case, it took us a full month to grant a developer administrator rights.

Additionally, it's not easy to gauge the quality of the transition. How do we gauge whether the knowledge sessions are really effective? How do we really know if we have understood everything? Any incumbent employee who has been working and supporting the system for a long time may well have established a few nifty things, such as little scripts or utilities for monitoring or promoting a piece of code, to make their jobs easier. Such things may not have been documented, but would aid in a lot of debugging issues and expediting delivery. Further, we may not see enough issues crop up to demonstrate all the measures used for maintenance and enhancements over a short span of time, whether through workshops or in the two to three weeks of shadowing and reverse shadowing.

In all cases, a stabilization phase continues over long periods. In my experience, and those of several colleagues who have taken over large enterprise platforms, it may take almost a year before you really feel in control and are operating at a level of optimized efficiency.

Post Takeover

The period after takeover always shows a dip in production availability and reliability. Teams go through long hours of stress as they battle production tickets and unknown areas of the application. Time taken to fix issues increases. Service organizations recognize this. Many contracts specifically ask for a waiver of penalty (or a holiday period) in the first few months on steady state. By the time teams feel in control, there is only a sigh of relief rather than joy. This period heavily tests the business and the relationships between organizations and amongst individuals. Some of my colleagues from ISVs have mentioned that the team literally slogs it out in the first year after takeover. Although many organizations are certified at SEI CMM Level 5, when a team hits a production snag, those certificates don't carry much weight. People need IT heroes in the team to pull things through. Dependencies on folks who are technically competent, can think on their feet, and can manage time pressures increase that much more. This has become de rigueur in today's knowledge transfer world.

Unfortunately, many times the outcome is not positive. Business impact can be huge when product performance is compromised. Older team members are called back, perhaps poached from other organizations, as desperate measures. Sometimes entire teams are replaced, creating, in a sense, a transition within a transition with far greater urgency. For many people, this becomes career limiting. Many senior level executives have lost their jobs when transitions have failed.

ITIL versus DevOps

Over the last few years, we have witnessed the industrialization of IT operations. ITIL[a] (Information Technology Infrastructure Library), a set of practices for IT service management (ITSM), has matured over the last five years. We now see the advent of automation in this space. Companies such as IPSoft[b] are using robots and artificial intelligence to support IT and business operations. These will continue to be relevant for large platforms running on COTS (commercial off-the-shelf) software implementations with limited customizations. In fact, with industrialization, we are seeing transitions mature and become more efficient in the COTS space.

Our world is hurtling relentlessly into a space where differentiated experiences and a quick time to market are becoming keys to survival. At the

a. http://searchdatacenter.techtarget.com/definition/ITIL
b. http://www.ipsoft.com/

(continued)

moment, there are quite a few differences between ITIL and DevOps. In order to aid this transition, I believe the ITIL paradigm will change to include key principles from the DevOps world:

1. DevOps takes a holistic view and stresses on the performance of the entire system. ITIL looks to break down the whole into phases of activities.

2. DevOps looks for a cross-disciplinary approach and stresses on outcome orientation. In the traditional ITIL set-up, there are clear compartments between Development and Operations. Even within operations, there are clear distinctions between Release Engineers, DBAs, Network Engineers, and Operations Staff.

3. DevOps tries to amplify feedback and continuously learn. The ITIL ethos follows planning control and documentation. ITIL tries to bring consistency by creating processes and checklists.

4. Both ITIL and DevOps use automation. In the case of DevOps, the focus is on automating routine tasks. With ITIL, artificial intelligence is being used to mimic human behavior.

To put it succinctly, the future of ITIL is one in which robots take over human activities. The ITIL paradigm (as does the Industrialization principle) looks to remove the uncertainties brought in by human interactions. In the DevOps world, on the other hand, the future looks to automate verifications done on the system by team members. DevOps and Agile celebrate the social angle of software development and maintenance.

Contracting

Enterprises are starting to recognize the need for longevity of key members. Today, customer organizations seek to get the names of key members put in the contract. Exit clauses in contracts are getting longer and longer. IT set-ups are learning the need to ensure continuity and cooperation in the case of handovers. There is an appreciation within enterprises that team transitions are becoming the norm rather than the exception. More than seven pages of a contract can be dedicated to engagement termination. These contracts touch upon various aspects from setting up transition managers and knowledge transfers to the rebadging of vendor personnel. Some contracts have even begun to require that client nominees be able to work from the vendor offices for purposes of transition. One must commend the proactive think-through on this subject at the contracting phase itself. The irony, though, is that organizations are trying to secure cooperation through contract negotiation.

Timing

A rush to complete transitions can have a detrimental effect. Let's take the example of banks. Bank activities are generally seasonal. Year-ends are crucial periods. Transitions in today's banks are planned so that teams do not "mess up" this crucial time. In effect, there is a rush to complete the transition before year-end activities begin. But what is often overlooked is that the new team is suddenly facing a set of crucial activities that they never had experience with. It's a bit like fielding the national squad for the World Cup with a set of players who have never played in a high profile and high pressure arena. No team has won the World Cup while fielding an entire squad of greenhorns. Instead, winning teams always have a judicious mix of youth and experience. Similarly, in the case of transitions, is it not better to have the new team pair up with the incumbent on an activity as critical as this, rather than relying on the new team's untested skills and capabilities to pull through?

Scope

Today's knowledge transfer focuses on taking over the support and maintenance of an application. However, no focus is given on how teams should work to enhance the application. Development is different from support. The exercise of inception to working with business on showcasing stories is unique to every organization. In three months, which is about the duration of today's transition agreements, many teams don't get an opportunity to partner with the incumbent and deliver an enhancement. Imagine a scenario when the old team is no longer around and the new team is tasked with an enhancement. They meet the business folks and they are told "that's not how we do it here," or worse, "that's not how the old team used to run this." That can make the situation quite awkward, and things can quickly decline from there.

Today's Transition Program Manager

Suresh is an experienced IT program manager working for a large service organization. He has been working in the IT industry for over fifteen years. He has led several successful transitions in his career. When his team contracts with a new account, they identify large development projects expected ahead of time. Then, they request the incumbent to complete these projects. Because Suresh's team will have their hands full taking on the maintenance aspects of the existing platform, they don't have time to focus on the new projects. Suresh realizes that this goes against the grain of practical wisdom. The new projects drive innovation. New projects will have more maintenance and enhancement challenges after they go live. Yet his team continues to focus on the matured systems even as work in progress (WIP) streams do not attract any focus.

Organizations are particularly keen to understand how to transfer over projects that have been developed in an Agile fashion into maintenance mode, and they are asking this specific question to the service organizations they hire. No one has really broached this topic in-depth. This is primarily because development phases have picked up Agile models, whereas, in many instances, the maintenance and operations teams work with older methods. Consider the case of a colleague who was coming out of a large-scale transition of a development project into operations. In this case, the biggest challenge he faced was that every time the development phase needed to handover to operations, they began hitting roadblocks. Operations would say that adequate documentation was not present to take over the application. The development team would say that a working product is more important than comprehensive documentation.[1] Both development and operations view things from different positions on Agile adoption. In an ideal world, the operations team would have been involved with the project from the requirements and development phase. On the flip side, the expectations of the operations team would have been factored into every story played by the development team. A few organizations are beginning to restructure this into a DevOps model.[2] The DevOps model focuses on both development and operations with the intent to provide continuous delivery. To put it in another way, in this paradigm, development and IT operations happen continuously and seamlessly. However, the vast majority of organizations still do not operate with this philosophy.

True Cost of Transfer

A related issue to knowledge transfer is its limitations on business advancement. Many organizations have a tendency to pause project development while knowledge transfer is in progress. It is understood that projects may be paused for about three months. However, in reality, the impact is much longer. The entire stabilization period slows down delivery. New features and functionality may not reach the market on time. This adversely impacts the competitiveness of the organization, which may be the very reason why a transfer was triggered in the first place. This is another phase in which the relationship between business and IT is tested immensely. The confidence in IT decreases within the organization. Apart from the obvious issues of delivery slow-down, IT members may fail to have the right levels of context and domain understanding to engage with business members effectively. This leaves business members spending more time with the added task of detailing out functionalities and expectations for the IT members. Business members will also

---

1. http://agilemanifesto.org/
2. https://en.wikipedia.org/wiki/DevOps

need to acutely focus on testing out the new features with the new team. However, none of the knowledge transfer metrics currently track these impacts.

For too long, we have focused on the operational efficiency of IT projects as opposed to their effectiveness. The project charter goes through deliberate discussions on the purpose of the project. Most projects quantify the expense and the expected benefits of doing the project. A business case is put out to justify the return on investment (ROI). After this has been approved, everyone focuses on staying within the cost, timeline, and scope of the project. We often do not step back to see whether the real purpose of the project is still relevant or whether there might be other opportunities along the way. The metrics on knowledge transfer continue to focus on operational aspects such as how much has been transferred, the cost incurred so far, and the team's ability to stick to their deadlines. We don't try to determine how well things have been transferred. So although we can have a lot of "completed" tick marks, true internalization hardly ever occurs. We get what we measure. Unfortunately, in this case, we aren't measuring the right stuff.

The inherent costs of a transfer run much deeper than the time and effort spent directly on the activities. Costs of business disruption after the handover or during the stabilization phase can be debilitating. However, these costs may not be directly attributed to the knowledge transfer, often because the project may have been "completed" by then. The opportunity costs of failing to put functionalities in the market can be quite heavy. Needless to say, the ecommerce world is rapidly evolving. Competition exists in every sphere and customers are getting savvy and demanding. One can ill-afford to pause innovation that customers look for. Such costs are rarely accounted for within the metrics tracked on a knowledge transfer project. These costs can be several times higher than the direct cost of personnel in the project.

Agile software development has seen substantial adoption among organizations. Agile and Lean delivery focus on high-engaging, non-fussy models to deliver software. Most importantly, the cultural shift in the Agile model requires a substantial people-centric approach. Today, many software platforms are developed using Agile methodologies. More importantly, there are several benefits in utilizing Agile philosophies when undertaking knowledge transfer programs. Agile focuses substantially on business outcome versus operational efficiency, on quicker outcomes along with quicker material feedback. Agile also does not focus on "big bang" releases. Instead, it encourages us to release in short cycles, allowing us to refine our processes and get feedback. Adopting a similar approach to knowledge transfer would allow us to reap the very same benefits. Smaller milestones allow the team to get quick wins, increasing confidence all around. It also allows us to learn and adapt. This is even more crucial in a project whose execution will be nebulous. These projects will witness heavy undercurrents given teams from different groups are involved. This is all the more reason to give such projects more time to think big while starting small.

Practical World

Many of my friends and colleagues work in the IT industry. Many work in service organizations and quite a few work in IT groups of large corporations. We have had several discussions on the concept of ownership and with every conversation, a new challenge arises. The real world is far murkier than the pristine idealism of cooperation and partnership.

Competing Priorities

These days, customers commonly ask for key project personnel to be mentioned in the contract. However, a "seasoned" service organization manager would never put his stars on that list. In fact, delivery managers take pride in ensuring that the real performers of the team do not get caught into the contract trap. The moment the incumbent team's management realizes that they are losing business, they will focus all their efforts on finding new pastures where better business opportunities may exist. This is a classic case of competing priorities. In an Agile paradigm, teams need to spend time in handing over ownership, but if the parent organization of the incumbent has a conflicting interest and seeks to pull out key members, this will never occur. There are no easy answers to this practical problem, and most often, the issue cannot be resolved using contracts. Customer organizations need to think from the viewpoint of the incumbent vendor and understand what would appeal to them and keep them on-board. In our case, the EuroT CIO himself suggested that we use this exercise as a way to build a center of excellence on knowledge transfer. That sounded ambitious to many of us. Some of us had already experienced knowledge transfers in prior engagements, but the opportunity to look upon this as a discipline in itself and elevate it to a higher order added a new level of enthusiasm. Since then, we have carried over what we have learned as we moved on to other engagements.

Rebadging

A transition often means hiring some of the employees from the incumbent organization. The industry-accepted term for this is *rebadging*. Rebadging derisks the program and application to a great extent. However, rebadging can also have its pitfalls. Employees may not be ready for a rebadge. The good ones may find better options and move on. In most cases, employees may not be happy with a move from a customer organization to a vendor organization, for example, or across vendors. Personal equations and egos get in the way. Eventually these people quit, taking their knowledge with them.

However, rebadging has become an accepted norm. Many of my colleagues vouch for the efficacy of this practice. In reality, what these organizations are doing is buying more time for their intended team to build context. The members who have been rebadged will go through a completely different transition—a new organization, a new culture, and perhaps a different career path. Many may have transferred to the incumbent because it seemed to be the safest option at that time; but most will reconsider.

A client with an Agile organizational culture would have a fairly sound idea of the real performers from the incumbent. The incumbent management runs the risk of losing some of these employees if the client or the new vendor decides to make offers. These types of situations can become lose-lose very quickly. Therefore, it's in everyone's interest to sit down and make a commitment to make the transfer successful.

Story of a Rebadged Employee

Sunita worked at the Mumbai center of MegaTos, the technology division of Mega, Inc., a global leader in the banking world. She was a young IT engineer with about two-and-a-half years of experience. She was one of those team members who jumps in and solves problems with verve and vigor. She enthusiastically volunteered for all activities, be it testing, analyzing logs, or comparing features across environments. She was part of a 2,500 member IT group. In November 2010, they were informed that their entire division was to be merged with Vettai, Inc., a large India-based services provider employing over a hundred thousand people. The merger was to happen within three months. By January 2011, all 2,500 members would be employees of Vettai, Inc.

In the beginning, everything was the same. Sunita went through the induction processes from Vettai, Inc. Like everyone else in her IT group, she got the joining kit and had a sense of being made welcome. Even after January, the members of the IT group continued to receive their salaries in the MegaTos format with their MegaTos ID. Their Vettai email IDs had not been set-up. Not that it mattered to Sunita. The location was the same, the facility managements were the same and nothing really changed until May of 2011.

Sunita noticed that the fifteen members of senior management from MegaTos had resigned. The CEO of MegaTos had left in January. Given her profile and the nature of her work, this did not make any direct difference to her. However, other things began to bother her. MegaTos had implemented a product from DhanTech, Inc. Of late, the consultants from DhanTech had become less responsive to her. DhanTech had removed certain access privileges she had enjoyed earlier, making her feel handicapped. She was no longer their client, but a partner vendor.

(continued)

In the first week of June of 2011, as the employees were walking in to work, security replaced their MegaTos badges with Vettai badges. This was a full five months after the transition was supposed to be completed. The merger had finally become a reality in their world.

At Vettai, Sunita started to feel like she had to prove herself all over again. Vettai, Inc. was a 150,000-employee behemoth. Rewards and recognition systems were vastly different from what she had known. At MegaTos, the employees received a bonus based on the company's performance. At Vettai, their bonus was driven based on the performance of many other projects and accounts, teams that Sunita had no clue about. At MegaTos, she could work from home when required. All she needed to do was inform everyone by email. At Vettai, she had to request it in advance and her request had to be approved by a manager.

Sunita was married at the end of 2011. She wanted a transfer to Pune, a city 150 kilometers from Mumbai, since her husband worked out of that city. Fortunately, Vettai, Inc. had a thriving work center in Pune. She put in a request and was fortunate enough to get a work allocation to the Pune office. However, her first day at Pune office in January 2012 proved to be a shock. Outside of the Mumbai office, she was not recognized as an employee anywhere else within the Vettai internal systems. Her access card did not work. She had to prove to security that she was actually an employee. She learned that the 2,500 employees retained from MegaTos had been tagged as an XT044 group whereas the regular Vettai employees were XT01. She required a company bus for her commute. But with her XT044 tag, she could not take advantage of that benefit. Whenever she needed to work late into the night, she had to use the cab facility, but she did not have access to raise the request.

A year after the announcement of the transition, Sunita had transitioned out of MegaTos, but she had not been transitioned into Vettai, Inc. For the next five years, former MegaTos employees were not allowed to work on any other project within Vettai, Inc. Within three years, the formerly 2,500 strong MegaTos group had shrunk to 150 members. Eventually, Vettai, Inc. closed down the Mumbai office, the building that had housed the erstwhile MegaTos office.

The Evolving Nature of the Program

Areker Bank is one of the largest banks in the U.S. Their current banking platform, named Lothar, has been running for the last thirty years. Over time, their customer demographics began to change. Customers had become more connected, empowered, and demanding. The bank implemented a next-generation banking product to serve this new-age customer—Banker, a product of Sofa Technologies, one of the largest software companies in the world. This program was christened as Nerup.

Areker planned to utilize Agile methodologies for the implementation. They took over direct responsibility for implementing Banker from Sofa. Areker engaged LeanAgile, Inc. in the transition program. The plan was for LeanAgile to take over the Banker product implementation from Sofa within a span of six months, but as the engagement progressed, they realized that Sofa Technologies brought deep product knowledge, something that neither Areker nor LeanAgile would be able to pick up within six months. Because this was still a fairly new product, only personnel within Sofa technologies had enough knowledge of the product to effectively implement it. Such skills were not available elsewhere in the market.

As this realization dawned on the parties, they extended their engagement with Sofa Technologies. The teams have now been working on Banker implementation for more than two years. Even to this day, the implementation team is largely comprised of Sofa engineers. They were able to change course because at some level they were following the Lean principle to defer commitment.[3] This principle states that decisions must be frozen as late as possible in the process, especially those decisions that become irreversible. If they had made up their minds to take over and sealed down contracts and timelines accordingly, the banking system would have crashed, and most likely Areker Bank would have gone out of business.

Politics

Most IT organizations take a radically different approach than what Areker Bank chose. Knowledge transfer often begins with a surreptitious agreement between the customer and the new vendor. This period sees heavy negotiations. The client is keen to get good rates and a robust set of SLAs (service level agreements).[4] The vendor is keen to win the business. All of the negotiations are centered around rates, the SLAs, and how soon one can take over. In effect, all of the negotiations are about improving

---

3. www.allaboutagile.com/7-key-principles-of-lean-software-development-2/
4. http://searchitchannel.techtarget.com/definition/service-level-agreement

IT efficiency. There is little to no focus on business outcome. The vendor uses their prior knowledge with similar engagements to negotiate. The client uses their historical experience with the incumbent to negotiate. All through the process, both IT parties overlook the purpose of the product.

Unfortunately, these discussions and the negotiated contract are what drive team behavior. Given the need for discretion, both the client and vendor make many assumptions about the product and the environment in which it will be used. The vendor is most interested in winning the account and making a sustained profit on the account. The IT organization is looking to drive down costs and maintain SLAs. Teams are trained to show their SLAs are within limits. If the product fails, it could be marketing's fault or the business team's mistake because they did not know what their customer wanted. However, the IT organization and the vendor are happy if they are within their SLAs.

After the contract is signed, the onus is upon the incumbent. The obvious reflex is to resist and turn hostile. Even if the technical team on the ground is open to help, the incumbent's management might make it as difficult as possible. The incumbent account manager might be worried about his job. Last-ditch efforts are made to win back confidence. A number of concessions are provided. However, given that the client and the new vendor have signed what is considered a rock-solid contract, there is no wiggle room for the incumbent. When this becomes obvious, the incumbent management may lose interest. They might try to pull out their best members to focus on "rising accounts." And so, all of the team's and management's energy goes into getting everyone to interact in a productive manner. Driving this behavior creates a lot of waste in the system. Nine times out of ten, the clauses mentioned in the contract will fall through. The SLAs become unachievable. Many of the original assumptions turn out to be wrong. The product suffers.

Losing Incumbent Members – A Different Perspective

The Banker Product skill is very much in demand. A number of Sofa engineers have quit the Nerup program. This poses a risk to the transition. However, the Areker management took a unique perspective on this. They believe that with their in-house team and the LeanAgile team going through the transition, they are actually better placed and more secure for the future. In effect, Areker Bank believed that the incumbent personnel would, in any case, have moved on at some point.

Things to Know and Do

- Program schedules can be unrealistically short given the operational challenges to execute such programs.

- The true cost of transfer includes the opportunity cost of missed projects and revenue loss due to increased service disruptions.

- The focus on transitions is often on efficiency and not effectiveness. There is a greater focus on activity over outcomes.

- Scope may be focused only on maintenance and not enhancements. This gives no opportunity to prioritize what needs to be transitioned and what doesn't.

- Politics may creep in between the three groups: IT management, the incumbent team, and the new team.

- The program may evolve differently from what was envisioned. Watertight contracts do not provide wiggle room to course-correct the transition.

Chapter 2

Ownership Transfer: Bringing Home a Child

I am the proud father of two lovely children, a boy and a girl. When our first child entered our lives, my wife and I were ecstatic. We went to the hospital as two people and came out as three. The first few moments were ones of relief that slowly transformed to bliss. Over the next two days, the baby was taken care by the hospital staff. We were around for all the good things—cuddling the baby, watching it opening its eyes, seeing a nurse give him a bath, and so on. After we reached home, our lives turned upside down. Things we hadn't even thought about in the normal course of events suddenly stood out as risky or dangerous. We actually had to give him a bath and change nappies on our own. Hold a newborn whose neck is not set yet and try giving him a bath. Your every heartbeat gets amplified. Your hands may shake. You begin to wonder if the water is too hot or too cold. Also, the baby would howl for long periods of time. The first few times, we did not even know why he was howling. Feeding would not always pacify him. We were not sure what to do. We never missed anyone the way we missed the nursing staff on that day.

I could not really put my finger on it for a while, but things had become very different. My cousin put it to me starkly when he had a baby. He called me and said, "You know, Vinod, after the baby I am a second citizen at home." That statement really brought home the enormity of the situation. As a parent, your time is not yours anymore. Your priorities are subservient to someone else's. Your likes and dislikes do not matter anymore.

When our second child was due, we felt a lot more comfortable. We had already experienced bringing home a baby. But this time, three of us went in and came out as four. Our six-year-old son brought a new dimension to our lives. But now we worried whether our newborn would compromise the attention we gave to our elder child. A lot of expectation-setting and counseling preceded the actual event, but it was still not the same after the second baby came home. We had to divide our attention between our son's schooling and our newborn's needs. However, all of these hardships are worth the experience of watching our children grow.

It goes against the grain of practical wisdom, but the best place for a child is with her parents. The staff of a hospital or an orphanage has more knowledge of how to take care of a baby. There are people with experience, doctors with degrees who would know just what is required. A hospital has nutritionists who know what to feed a child and how much. People in the orphanage have enormous experience in raising children. Yet we all know that the best place for a child is her parent's home. Parents take ownership and invest in giving the best life for their child.

My wife and I may not know everything about caring for a child, but we learn both from our own experiences and from those of others. We observe keenly, worry (sometimes needlessly) and, in general, take any and every measure to provide the best life for our child. When you bring home a baby, you do not just leave the hospital and bring it home. You need to prepare first. You need to purchase a crib, a car seat, blankets, clothes, and a range of other things. You then need to reorganize your routines. Your sleeping patterns and your work schedule may change. You may need additional help for a while. It takes quite a bit of organization to adjust your lifestyle when a new baby is brought home.

It's not very different with an application. You need to organize things before bringing the application into your workplace. Just knowing what the application does will not suffice. You need to have created the right environment, the right infrastructure; the right processes, and the right bandwidth before bringing in the application.

Ownership Is More than Experience and Expertise

Ownership is an indeterminate quality whose value overshadows many other qualities, including knowledge and experience. Knowledge, for instance, is useful, but it's not always necessary to know everything; often it's enough to know where to look for an answer. Experiences are amorphous. They evolve and register as composites. Your memories of an event can evolve over time, or can be influenced by other people. Two people's takeaways from the same experience can be dramatically different. Hence, project experience is often overrated. The doctor may say the same thing to both parents on how to rear the baby, but each follows the doctor's instructions in his or her own way.

Investment

Ownership grows with investment. Most parents would agree that the magic of parenthood did not occur the moment they first set eyes on their baby. The baby looked like any other baby. The first few days are often a literal shock, especially for first-time parents. Even second- or third-time parents still need to make a lot of adjustments. Bonds develop over time depending on the time, effort, and emotion invested in the baby. It doesn't matter whether it's your biological baby or an adopted one. Investment is key.

Empowerment

I believe we did a major disservice to this discipline by calling it *knowledge* transfer. Ownership is a lot more than just knowledge. The traditional way of looking at ownership involves such terms as responsibility and accountability, but neither of those involve empowerment. Ownership demands empowerment. As parents, we are empowered to decide and act on what is best for our child. Beginning from the food it takes to the school the child goes to, parents know that they have the final say in fulfilling their child's needs. Similarly, when you take over an application, you must not only maintain the application, you must also evolve the application according to the times. This may require adding enhancements at some times, pruning at other times, and perhaps even finally retiring the application. The team should feel it has the freedom to make the changes it deems fit for the best of the product.

Building Ownership Takes Time

Taking ownership requires a deep appreciation of expectations and empowerment. If you try to live by others' expectations, then ownership becomes compromised. Someone truly passionate about her application will work for the best possible outcome no matter what others think. True ownership shows by itself. You need not talk about it.

But how can you ensure true ownership develops? True ownership will develop only through deliberate intent. You have to spend time with the application: Work with the application. Enhance it. Prune it. Release it. Make mistakes. Discover little nuggets of code that can still surprise you. Invest your personal attention to the code. This shift in approach is all in the mind and not so much in practice. That is why it is extremely important for an ownership transfer event to occur over a considerable period of time. Having personal stories around the code and functionality is an excellent way to identify whether ownership is developing.

Action

If the team continues to blame the previous team for mistakes in the code, you can be certain that true ownership has not occurred. If her child misbehaves at school, a parent will not simply blame the teacher. A parent's first priority is her child. This may involve discussing matters with her son, with his teacher, or perhaps even changing schools. But simply blaming without acting helps no one. Ownership, therefore, involves action.

The Renter's Mindset

The Puba Boulevard community in Bangalore has more than a thousand flats. More than seventy percent of them are rented out. The tenants there make considerable contributions to the community. However, when a problem occurs within the community, the most a tenant tends to do is inform the owner or write a complaint to the association manager.

The Puba Resident's association started painting the exteriors to the apartments. This was a community-driven activity. Apart from the funds collected, lots of volunteer work was required to make this a success. However, painting apartments is an intrusive job. People would need to park their vehicles in other locations, remove their belongings from the balcony, and take different routes to enter and exit the apartment community. Accordingly, volunteers posted many notices informing everyone what was going to happen.

Many tenants had satellite dishes or air conditioners on their balconies. As the painting progressed, drops of paint fell on some of this equipment. The volunteers had not thought to mention the need to cover dishes or air conditioners in the signs they posted, but even so, tenants hadn't taken it upon themselves to protect their belongings either. When complaints began pouring into the association, they were predominantly from tenants and not from the owners. Further, the owners often either provided suggestions to deal with the problem or volunteered to modify the notices posted in the neighborhood. This attention to detail shows that the level of ownership for an owner is much greater than that of a tenant.

How Do You Recognize Ownership?

Ownership is a state of mind. There is no objective way to measure someone's level of ownership. However, human beings have a great ability to take up ownership when they feel it's needed. This ownership shows in the interactions and behavior of the individual and the team.

We can find different approaches to ownership among people at work. Some volunteer for an activity and then work on it until they identify the first roadblock. After they have identified the problem, they highlight it, ensure everyone understands it—and then go quiet. They then wait for someone to come and tell them that the impediment has been removed. This is a clear indication of lack of ownership. Someone who is truly interested in solving the problem will persist, follow-up, and volunteer to remove impediments until the problem is resolved. Intent and action are often far more important than skill and expertise.

If the new team asks questions like "how do you address 'x' problem", or "what will you do if we get into 'y' situation," then we are going in the right direction. But if the new team starts off by saying, "this is not possible" or "that's not how we do this here," then we are looking at a long and perhaps expensive engagement to transfer ownership. In a world that is hurtling towards being Agile, principles and commitments become far more important than accountability and responsibility. Commitment (or lack thereof) is never easy to measure and sometimes even to sense. Different levels of feedback are required to ensure we understand the pulse on the ground.

It's never easy to build ownership. It's unrealistic to expect that the receiving team will jump with joy about taking on new responsibility. In some cases, individuals already have more than enough on their plate. You can dance around the details, explain to the teams that more people are coming in to help or that some of their responsibilities will get rearranged, but the fact of the matter is, this new application adds an extra dimension to each person's sphere of responsibility. Which parent-to-be has not experienced anxiety when they learned they were to have a baby? The added responsibility and commitment, and the simple fear of the unknown can be overwhelming. Taking on a new application is not very different, though it is much smaller in magnitude. This makes it very important for leaders to sit down and explain to those involved why taking on this new responsibility is necessary and how it will help them grow. There needs to be a full understanding of the goal within the unit across the board. Team members need to accept that this change is occurring and is in a sense inevitable. Eventually, you can expect a switch in their mindset from the drawbacks of this new responsibility to the ensuing possibilities.

When the discourse moves onto the receiving team giving ideas on making things better, you know that the right climate has set in. But it's quite important to recognize these winds of change. Agile helps a lot in creating the right environment because it requires strong team bonds and a highly empowered team. A positive and motivated team environment often catalyzes creation of ownership. In the book, *How Will You Measure Your Life?*, Clayton M. Christensen and his coauthors James Allworth and Karen Dillon include a chapter on what makes people tick.[1] One telling aspect they

---

1. http://www.claytonchristensen.com/books/how-will-you-measure-your-life/

touch upon is that the greatest motivation is often the journey itself, the richness of experience, and just being part of a motivated and happy team. Agile allows you to create such a team. This symbiosis is illustrated in this famous fable, which is frequently used when discussing the principles of Agile.[2]

> A pig and chicken are walking on the road when the chicken says, "Hey Pig, I think we should open a restaurant."
>
> The pig thinks about it for a while and says, "Hmm. It sounds like a good idea, but what shall we call it?"
>
> The chicken says: "Let's call it 'Ham and Eggs.'"
>
> The pig quips: "I don't think so. I'd be committed, but you would be only involved."

In the case of EuroT, this principle played out in London at an early point. The initial discussions were not going well for the program manager, Lisa. She was trying to align with the delivery managers of each team. However, every step of the way, she received a number of questions and excuses. Many reasons were given as to why something was risky or why Path A should be chosen instead of Path B. Meetings were hard and long. They could reach no consensus about who would take ownership for the various pieces of the project. There finally came a point when Lisa told the delivery managers, "Here is the budget identified for the program. Now you sit and decide how you want to spend it, and who will take ownership for what." They arranged a separate session that Lisa did not attend. Decisions were made in that meeting and, in Lisa's own words, things became much smoother from there on. Because the teams got to choose for themselves, the level of ownership on the program itself increased that much more. In a sense, the teams must have felt that they were the pigs who would be committed to living with the components. The ownership transfer program and its manager were the chicken. After this program is complete, they would move on to other things.

Many times, we do not anticipate all the challenges involved. Years ago, during ThoughtWorks' early days, we had to transfer a fairly large e-commerce application over to an American digital retailer. Our team tried to explain the intricacies involved, the importance of application response times, and the way we ensured functional integrity using automated test cases. They listened to us and, after a mere three weeks, said they were confident in their ability to take over the application. So, we moved on from the project.

Six months later, our chief operating officer received a call from the same client. The client ranted about what a shoddy job we had done with the application and what an even worse job we had done with the transfer. The application was having lots of issues. Releases were long and the application had also become extremely

---

2. http://www.agilejedi.com/chickenandpig

slow. When we investigated, we discovered that most of the principles of engineering and design we set up had been violated. The new team had completely dismantled the build setup as it was coming in their way. The previously automated builds had not been working for six months. Because we were away from the scene, we had been made into the scapegoat for everything that had gone wrong. But the larger issue was what had become of the application. To continue with the parenting metaphor, a new mother would not necessarily blame the hospital and allow their baby to be sick. Rather, she would call the hospital to find out how to cure the baby and then seek advice on how to ensure the baby thrives. This should also be the case for problems that arise following an application transfer.

With the EuroT program, we had the maturity to realize that it might take a couple of months to transfer knowledge. But ownership is a lot more than knowing. We pledged to be engaged until ownership moved over. The Bangalore team continued to display ownership for the application. After all, they had invested five years of their lives in bringing the application to its current state. The London folks cultivated ownership over time. Every story, every defect, and every release gave them experience with the application. Each of those experiences allowed them to become more confident and to develop a personal stake in the application. Time and experience had generated ownership.

Things to Know and Do

- Ownership is more than knowledge and experience.
- Ownership demands empowerment.
- Ownership triggers action.
- Ownership is difficult to be measured objectively. It can only be sensed.
- Building ownership requires investment of time and effort.

Chapter 3

The Approach

Ownership transfer needs to be planned and executed. Given the myriad patterns and dimensions of such exercises, it is difficult to create a catchall template for these programs. Our transfer exercise with EuroT is an example of one of our very successful transfers.

I don't know of many other instances where the client director asks the incumbent to devise a plan to transfer their work to a new team. It's a grand testament to the strong relationship that EuroT and ThoughtWorks had built over time. This approach gave the program a unique vantage point and allowed us to create an approach keeping the best interests of the EuroT application in mind. There were no other undercurrents to watch out for. Sometimes, the best way is the most direct.

After the idea of the transfer had been internalized, we could sit down and think about getting our hands around this initiative. This is a nebulous activity. The end of the exercise does not really produce a "thing." Software, by its very nature, is intangible and doesn't produce something that can be touched or felt. However, in many cases, we can see a new feature, an extra field that is needed, or a smoother user experience. But in the case of knowledge transfer, the outcome is generally invisible to the end users.

Visualize the To-Be State

The team spent some time trying to visualize the end goal, which, as it turned out, could be visualized in many different ways. One approach was to look at what work would still be left in Bangalore. Was the expectation to move everything to London?

Mason (the director) had left that open. While the overall ask was to move things over, we did not want to bite off more than we could chew. Because the application was the soul of the organization, we needed to ensure that EuroT's customers continued to receive the same, if not better, level of service and availability as before. If that meant we needed to have some support continue out of Bangalore, we were prepared to do so. Needless to say, this created high levels of uncertainty for the program team, but on the positive side, it offered an opportunity for the team to create the future.

Another thing to consider is how the move will affect the client and where there are opportunities to improve. One is the obvious cost savings in reducing the number of team members. But it is naive to think of it is as simply passing over knowledge and decreasing the team size. People are not just sitting and twiddling their thumbs or waiting to be told what to do next. Every member of a team has some work to do all the time. Ask any member of an IT team what is on their plate, and he or she would probably have at least five items on a to-do list. Some of the tasks could be redundant and some could be optimized, but many of those activities are genuinely critical. The end state needs to reflect how the structure and process of delivering projects and maintenance of the application would change in the new world.

Lastly, the team needs to look at infrastructure. After more than seven years of distributed development, many procedures were set up in Bangalore. We had contracted with an Indian data center to provide us virtual machines on request. We had created an elaborate setup for running our development shop as well as functional testing and performance testing. In the new world, would this infrastructure get transferred to London? Or, because we are working in a virtual world, should the data center continue out of Bangalore? With a smaller team, do we even need the entire infrastructure? This discussion proved to be very useful. Each of these dimensions translated into specific areas for planning and execution.

We had a vision of the future, but that did little to help us take off. During a discussion with the teams, a developer asked us, "What about code?" It was a moment of epiphany. Working code had to be at the center of this program. Everything else—process, structure, infrastructure—is worthless without working code. And so it was that we picked up one end of the thread. From there, it was easy to categorize logical chunks of the technical architecture. These formed the knowledge units for the transfer.

As we broke down the technical architecture into knowledge units, it became clearer and clearer that appreciating the code in its raw format would only go so far for the new team to take charge. We needed to think of how the new setup would impact development and code fixes. We also needed to transfer knowledge on how the code was written, refactored, and propagated across environments. This is the engineering side of software development.

At a broad level, we had identified four different streams to address in this exercise: code, engineering, infrastructure, and process. And unlike templated knowledge transfer exercises, we had looked upon this as a change management exercise. After seven years of working together, we knew the challenges of taking ownership. There are two different organizations at play. The exercise involves individuals from different countries. Culture plays a huge role throughout the exercise and beyond.

Things to Know and Do

- Visualize the end state.
- Understand the different dimensions involved—namely code, process, engineering, and infrastructure.
- Feed these dimensions into the program plan.

Chapter 4

The Program

Purpose of the Program

Ownership transfer is not an end in itself. The transfer is happening to serve a larger purpose. This purpose needs to be articulated. In the case of EuroT, the program was christened as a "transformation program." This term embodied all of the different expectations of the exercise. From a team of 150 members across both geographies, we were coming down to about 60 members and perhaps in a single geography. This called for a different set of competencies to run the program. It would call for changes to the team structure, merging of responsibilities amongst teams, and even changes to day-to-day practices. This was a much larger paradigm than just knowledge transfer.

The transformation phrase elevates this exercise beyond the four walls of two teams undertaking knowledge transfer. The transformation involves a change on how the IT organization is run. Equally important is what it means to the operations of the entire organization. Daily interactions between the business teams and the IT teams would change. By involving all parties, we created an opportunity for all stakeholders to determine the future.

Because we called it a "transformation program," the outlook was not limited to the immediate activity. It focused on the eventual steady state situation. Given my earlier experiences on similar cases, we would have either termed it a downsizing activity, or a knowledge transfer exercise. It would have been handled within a closed group. Other departments would have known about the exercise only on an as-needed basis.

The Vanishing IT Member

Tom, a marketing manager at PaperBed Incorporated, sent an email to one of his partner members, Ajay, in their IT department. He was used to getting prompt responses from Ajay. This time, however, he did not get a response. Out of politeness, he waited for a week and subsequently sent reminder emails. When he still didn't get a response, he pursued the matter further. Two weeks after the first email, Tom discovered that Ajay, his IT friend, was no longer on the account. On top of it, Tom did not know who to reach out in Ajay's absence.

In most cases, we do not have a knowledge transfer exercise that is a pure "like for like" transfer. By this I mean the scope of the transfer is not such that hundred members replace hundred other members. We certainly do not execute "man-to-man" marking when taking over from the incumbent. These transfers are always linked with other strategic objectives. Everybody involved needs to understand the larger picture and the trigger for a transfer. In the case of EuroT, this communication and dialogue occurred through the entire organization. Most importantly, this purpose was shared with the incumbent as well as the new team members.

Orbits of Influence

As with any large program, we needed to identify stakeholders. Although some stakeholders are immediately obvious, we always miss those important ones who may not have an active participation, but whose cooperation is critical. We decided to map these stakeholders by their level of influence to the program (Figure 4.1). The ones in the center have the maximum influence and would also be impacted the most. As the orbits get larger their influence diminishes. This is what we term as Orbits of Influence. At EuroT, we initially identified the development teams as the primary stakeholders. After all, the transfer would occur from one development team to another. But who are the secondary stakeholders?

They really were the entire organization, from the commercial teams to the infrastructure support teams, operations, accounts, and even human resources. When we embarked on this program, we did not know immediately who would be impacted and how. The best way to start off would be to create orbits of influence. The development

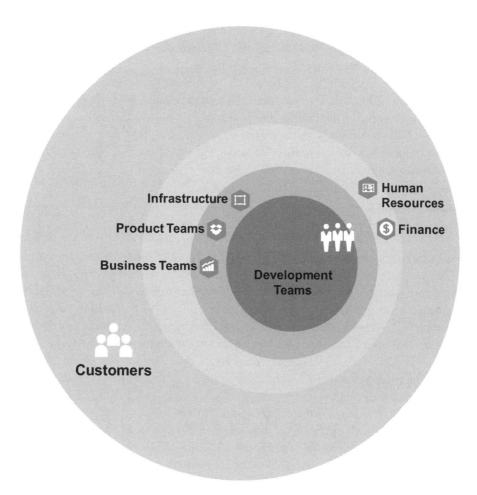

Figure 4.1 *Orbits of influence: departments influencing the transition program by primacy*

teams would be considered the nucleus. The closest orbit would be the IS and support teams. The development teams interact with the IS teams on a daily basis, whether it be for releases, production support, or even deployment-related challenges.

The next group contains all the business teams with which the team directly liaises for their project delivery. These could range from project managers to product owners. Depending on how an organization is structured, product owners could very well be in the center of the orbit as well.

Enabling teams may be considered key stakeholders, too. They are the members of the organization who provide support: human resources, finance, accounting, and administration. Ownership transfer involves people and responsibilities. Needless to say, some members are going to be personally impacted at the end of this project. It's important to keep morale high through the entire process. This is where the human resources department will need to play a major role.

Finance and accounting is impacted in two ways. Ownership transfer itself involves a cost. This needs to be accounted for and budgeted. The other angle is the cost of projects during the transfer and post-transfer. Many things will change during the program, starting with the platform, processes, and the people working on the application. It is to be expected that the cost of projects will also change. A reset of baselines will be required to define the new status.

Cost of the Program

We had initially identified the cost of this EuroT transformation at a million euros. Now, how does one estimate the cost of a transformation program? After all, this is unlike any other project. There is no historic precedent to refer back to. Using industry standards like function points or even story points (as defined for functional streams) will not work. One simply does not have a basis to assess the effort. Our biggest achievement was that we accepted this point almost immediately. We also accepted that any estimate may not be accurate. In this case, we broke down the program into what we termed KT (knowledge transfer) units. This was based on the current lay of the system.

But we also realized that there may be specific units focusing around process and tasks, activities such as production support, release activities, or functional streams that are relevant for the business analysts. We had automated the entire system. At its peak, we had about 6,000 automated tests running every day on the EuroT program. We optimized the tests over time to about 1000 tests running every day. Transfer would also require us to hand over quality assurance for the components.

Our estimate essentially relied upon asking senior developers and architects on how much time it would take to transfer over discrete KT units. We had to rely on the instincts of the Bangalore developers because the London teams opined that they had no way of knowing what they don't know. This is a matter of great sensitivity. The owner has to rely on the incumbent for how much effort she needs to put in. Trust and maturity are paramount in this exercise. The developers estimated in time. A unit would take x number of weeks or y number of months. This is in stark contrast to how regular transfers occur. The new team, a team that has not worked on the application at all, is asked for estimates. Whichever way a number is thrown, the client (or the management in cases of internal transfers) will negotiate on those numbers. It's a classic example of contract negotiation over customer collaboration. It's another matter entirely that both parties have little understanding of the complexity involved!

During the entire process, the running assumption was that someone from Bangalore would pair with someone from London. We had decided on remote pairing based on logistical as well as cost reasons. Processing visas as well as having the right set of individuals willing to travel is challenging. Some of these elements must be identified in advance. Remote pairing brings in its own level of inefficiencies. These need to be identified ahead of time, giving an opportunity for the developers to factor them in when estimating. As with all Agile concepts, we need to get individuals to sign up for such exercises. An ownership transfer exercise calls for team members with a high level of experience and maturity.

The next important factor was that pairing would not occur only to teach. Instead, pairing occurred to deliver functional projects. By functional projects, I mean projects whose purpose was to either increase revenues or bring down costs for the business. As the incumbent team, we were clear that learning happens best by doing, and not just by teaching. We created pairs to work on functional stories and ensured that these stories covered areas primarily around those that accounted for the KT unit's transfer. The question then became how to factor for costs. Our senior developers gave a sense of the "cost of transfer" while pairing on each story, not in monetary terms, but in the loss of productivity when playing the functional story. This loss of productivity was included in the transfer program budget.

Getting buy-in on this concept itself is a herculean task. This is when the stakeholders we talked to earlier come into play, especially the ones in finance. The managers whose projects become "guinea pigs" for the ownership transfer exercise become worried that work on the project may suffer. Stakeholder management is key during this transition. Because commercially significant projects are to be delivered, we need to keep the business groups in the loop. The traditional concept of project pricing takes a deviation when doing this transition. Part of the project cost goes to the business group sponsoring it, whereas another chunk goes towards the transition budget. It's easy for stakeholders to get into protracted discussions regarding costs. This is wasted energy. The best way to move forward is for senior management to keep all stakeholders informed at every major milestone and, more importantly, to convey what is expected in the ensuing months and how each group needs to participate in the transition.

The Scope

In the case of a functional program, it's easy to define scope. You know what functionality has to be realized and can work through the business value of a certain feature. It's not very different with ownership transfer. Before you start, a large project should be broken down into smaller manageable chunks. This is neither easy nor straightforward. The approach to dividing up the work on the application needs to suit the objective. We did not take the approach of breaking the code based on functionality. Working code is paramount. We broke down the code into discrete elements, keeping in mind how the system architecture has been defined. This step determines the entire direction of the ownership transfer. It has consequences on how teams work with the transferred code. Our end state of ownership had different teams owning components, but not functionality. Hence, breaking the code into components for transfer made sense. A different program may have an end state derived out of functionality. In that case, classification of the units could be different. Apart from the actual code, we also identified elements around processes and roles (release process for example) that needed to be transferred. Overall, we identified seventeen units to transfer.

Timeline

In most projects, timelines are determined by external factors. Perhaps there is a huge convention coming up that you need to be ready for. Maybe a regulatory change comes with mandated timelines, or you need to catch the sales cycle for a certain year. But for a program such as ownership transfer, you don't have an external factor determining the timeline. However, it's good to look at the timing of the transfer. It's useful to ensure that the transfer goes through key seasons during the process. This provides the new team an opportunity to experience the stress periods with the safety net of the incumbent's expertise. The timeline should also allow a few releases into production. Releases are always stressful periods and, in a sense, will reveal the maturity of the teams.

Most travel companies will see ticket sales peaking through the year-end holiday cycle. In the case of EuroT, we commenced the transfer activities in the early part of the year. Both teams witnessed five releases between them. By the time we reached the year-end, a good amount of the transfer was complete. However, we did have a small Bangalore presence during the year-end as well and both teams finished off the peak season together. The EuroT program also had intermediate milestones. Each of the KT units had to be transferred over in a given time. After they were transferred over, the London team took responsibility for handling those units. In parallel, some members from Bangalore left the project team, but only after one release with the relevant features went into production.

Program Structure and Governance

Being Agile is never an excuse for being unstructured. All Agile programs require a structure, a conscious mapping of stakeholders, and a governance mechanism to steer the program. Although we take great pride in saying the teams ought to do what they think is best and the scrum master (or iteration manager, or project manager, as the case may be) must remove impediments, we do not think enough about how the scrum master is enabled. If the scrum master is not empowered to talk to the right set of people and influence decisions, the project is doomed. That is where an appropriate structure and steering group is required. *Agile IT Organization Design* by Sriram Narayan provides a detailed illustration of how to set up organizations to embrace the Agile mindset.[1]

The question any CIO will need to answer is, "Who will run this program?" Because code is the essence of what is being transferred, the obvious choice would be someone within the development team. The problem with that is everyone in the development team also owns some element of the KT unit. Also, someone deeply embedded within the nucleus can be blinded by the details. The chances of missing the larger picture increases. In the case of the EuroT transition, we identified a program manager who was not intrinsically part of the development team, but was part of the business solutions team. She had experience working with the development teams and had the title of product owner for many critical features within the system, so she had a deep understanding of the application. She had also worked with most teams and interacted with many of the team members in her previous role. Hence we found that happy medium of having a level of familiarity, but not so close as to be blinded to the larger program.

Risks

Risk is often defined as all things uncertain. In the early stages of the program, we held a separate meeting with the EuroT CIO and discussed what could possibly go wrong. In that exercise, our intention was not to get through all of the risks and identify how to mitigate them. The EuroT CIO ran this meeting as a workshop with the sole purpose of identifying as many risks as possible. The consequences of these risks could be dealt with at a later time, if the need arose. As can be expected, many risks were identified. We came up with as many as 60 different areas of risk that touched upon all facets of the transformation.

We categorized these into seven areas. I am certain these risks will resonate with most transition exercises. Nomenclatures may change, but the themes should be consistent.

---

1. www.agileorgdesign.com/p/table-of-contents-preface.html

An Imperfect World

This was our way of stating that we are not handing over a perfect product. There will always be issues that will not be to the satisfaction of the new team. No application has zero faults. These faults often come to the forefront when a new team takes over. Differences of opinion arise on the reason for these faults. It is a challenge to identify the context on things that were not done right, but were done for a reason.

In the same vein, it is equally difficult for the incumbent to remember all of the minute technical details in the system and pass it on to the new team. In one of our earlier engagements, we had encountered several instances where the incumbent team was scared to modify an existing code because they did not know enough about it. This becomes all the more frustrating when addressing production issues.

An Imperfect System

Atozhotels.com is run by a hotel chain in the United States. The Web site provides revenues to the company of more than 5 billion dollars. Multiple hotel brands are run from the same platform. The IT team of this company, based in the US, used to put out releases every two weeks. Because they had a dual-site approach, part of their release strategy involved switching traffic to one of the data centers while upgrading the application version on another site. After testing the first site and ensuring everything was fine, they would redirect traffic to the first site and then upgrade the second site. The IT group traditionally had not followed a platform deploy for their application. Their releases essentially were glorified patch updates.

After several years, this team was required to hand the application over to their offshore center in Ukraine. There were several snippets of code and modules that confused the Ukraine team. They did not see a reason for the existence of those modules. The US team agreed with their Ukraine counterparts, but neither party had the confidence to delete the code. They just did not know what would break if the code gets deleted. In the maddening rush of releases every other week, the US team never had the chance to sit back and review these pieces of code. More than 50 percent of the code seemed unnecessary, but had to stay in the system because no one felt confident enough to make any changes.

The team taking over needs to have high levels of maturity to handle an imperfect world. More on this in Chapter 6 in the section, "'Not Invented Here' Syndrome."

Team Retention

This risk will exist in any ownership transfer program and is typically the elephant in the room. Most teams focus on the incumbent team being phased out after a time. However, during our transfer, we also discussed the role of the new team. Attrition of members of the new team can also be a point of risk. In the case of EuroT, this was a case of capacity transformation. We were in the unique situation of handing over additional responsibilities to a set of team members who already owned several modules within the organization.

Attrition is a big risk of all ownership transfer programs. The incumbent teams may quit or the new team members can find the situation too hostile and resign. We have already discussed the issue of rebadging in Chapter 1. Team retention is one of the softer aspects of this transition. I strongly suggest involving the HR team and senior executives to discuss this risk even before going ahead with the program.

In the case of EuroT, we had kept open the question of whether a team would eventually exist in Bangalore. While the primary reason was for support on production issues, this approach also helped from a capacity backup perspective.

Effectiveness and Assimilation

There is no easy way to measure the effectiveness of a transfer. We could certainly have created templates and checklists for activity completion. However, using classroom sessions or mere defect fixes will provide only limited value. The best way to internalize knowledge and context is by actually working on the module. One of the challenges we faced was that there weren't enough projects that would address all knowledge units. In hindsight, this should not have been a surprise. The reason for the capacity transformation was because the application feature set was stabilizing, which would mean that there would not be critical and priority requirements in all modules.

A further facet of this is knowledge assimilation. The new team needs to work on a project by themselves almost as soon as they have taken over. This allows the team to absorb and apply their learning and thereby enhance their confidence and competence. We noticed there weren't enough projects in the transferred modules a few months down the line as well. The EuroT executive leadership was tasked with the job of finding relevant projects for the teams to work on.

Management and Measurement

At a broad level, the EuroT team was moving towards an uncertain future without a clear definition of the outcome. From a measurement perspective, we did not have a clear way to confirm whether it was working. For most of us on the project, this type of a transition was a first-time experience. We did not have a history of successful transfer. We discuss more about measurement in Chapter 12, "Measuring Ownership Transfers."

In today's world of Lean and Agile, one year is a long time for any project. It can definitely bring its set of distractions and disruptions. Overall, it brings in high degrees of uncertainty:

- Management's focus on this activity can deviate.

- We may realize that the original budget is not adequate.

- If the schedule is impacted, it will have a direct bearing on the ramp-down plan.

- The EuroT transition program schedule was also linked to recruitments occurring for the onsite teams. If the recruitments do not go according to schedule, we may need to realign the transfer as well as roll-offs.

Motivation

Developers love to develop from scratch. Modifying someone else's code is not that interesting. But for most developers, modifying code is a necessary evil before they can advance in their careers. Similarly, people who are giving up ownership may have already moved on in their minds. Many incumbent members can be transferred to other projects. One senior IT manager told me that they often encourage their incumbent engineers to take vacations around the time of the transition. When they start on a new project, they need to give it their complete attention. There is also the practical issue of retaining focus on the transfer with other activities going on. The general tendency for the incumbent developers would be to focus on stories or issues coming up on those modules. In our case, the developers from London already had a set of responsibilities that also needed their attention.

In most cases, the reverse occurs: The incumbent is working on other projects in addition to the one being handed over. In a different transition exercise we undertook, the incumbent members were quite busy with a number of projects. They just did not have the motivation to pair with the new team.

Production Issues

Production issues are always the biggest worry for any IT organization. Service disruptions directly bleed money. At its peak, EuroT sells more than €500,000 in ticket sales every hour. Every hour of downtime leads to a loss of revenue as well as a potential loss of reputation and loyalty. Hence, the bare minimum expectation of a transfer is that the new team can handle production issues. Fixing production issues is not always that easy. Most organizations have a mature propagation path from development to test, stage, and production. If issues needed to be addressed, they would hopefully have been caught in a prior stage. If an issue shows up in production, it may be a unique scenario that had not been seen before that point. Some issues can't be replicated in other environments, and it can be difficult to debug issues directly in production. Even if a fix has been identified, propagating a patch into production calls for different competencies and skills mix. Production issues can take longer to address. Of course, if there are many production issues to fix, it provides the team many learning opportunities, but no IT manager worth his salt should hope for production issues!

Miscellaneous

We identified a number of other items that broadly fit into areas of process, skills, and organizational dynamics. One such area was how regular projects would be executed in the intervening period. Teams in Bangalore worked as feature teams, which meant that any team could pick up a feature and implement it. The EuroT teams in London followed more of a product approach. This meant that specific teams could make changes only to specific areas of the application. With a product approach, multiple teams would be involved in running a project. By its very nature, involving multiple teams increases the number of people involved in the conversation on any given project. Of course, in the long term, as teams develop expertise within their domains, their productivity often balances or even surpasses these communication overheads. But this is dependent on circumstances in that organization. Hence, the real question was whether transition to the new process would slow things down. Will the new process make projects more expensive? Some of these aspects will be discussed in Chapter 9, "Continuous Business."

As team structures began to change, the way projects were divided changed as well. Earlier stories were divided based on features. This often involved developing the user interface and the services involved as well as making database changes. With a product view, the services were handled by one team and the user interface by a different team. The real issue with this was with skill sets of the business analysts and the quality analysts. Are the business analysts technically skilled enough to define service stories? Are the testers technical enough to automate service stories and run them? These skill gaps are discussed in Chapter 13, "The Three Bridges."

One risk faced by our team was identified by the EuroT CIO, Dave. He recognized the potential for organizational politics to interfere with operations and how this would be manifested. When change occurs, people have a tendency to blame everything that goes wrong with that change. Teams on regular projects might blame the transfer exercise as a reason for delays and overshooting costs on their projects, regardless of how tangentially the transfer project might be related. There could also be a tendency to justify rising expenses as the cost of transfer. The risk of the transfer exercise picking up disproportionately high expenses was high. It was also a major reason for us to put a strong program management team in place.

Things to Know and Do

- The purpose of the program needs to be articulated. The purpose needs to focus on why the ownership transfer is occurring.

- The program needs to be structured ahead of time, with the right stakeholders involved.

- Create orbits of influence. The entire organization will be impacted by the program. Human resources will often play a key role because the program involves changes to the roles of people.

- Involve the incumbent engineers to understand complexity and effort.

- Run a candid session to identify all potential risks for the program.

Chapter 5

Being Agile

The fundamental philosophies of Agile are enshrined in the Agile Manifesto. It states,

> Individuals and interactions over processes and tools
> Working software over comprehensive documentation
> Customer collaboration over contract negotiation
> Responding to change over following a plan
> That is, while there is value in the items on the right, we value the items on the left more.

Being Agile is perhaps one of the more important aspects of an ownership transfer exercise. After all, in these cases, we often begin exercises with nebulous expectations of the outcome. Teams are eclectic collections of individuals gathered from different organizations. Strong undercurrents and conflicting objectives can drive team behavior. In such situations, one needs to be flexible with the approach while not compromising the end vision. In effect, plan big, but act small.

Pairing Interaction and Collaboration

Software development is largely dependent on human involvement. In the case of ownership transfers, these are more pronounced than ever. If people do not cooperate in this exercise, the entire endeavor can be doomed. The process of remote pairing strikes right at the root of focusing on individuals and interactions. At EuroT, we conducted norming sessions to enable members from London to feel part of the Bangalore team. Having done that and established a level of comfort, we left it to the developers to run with the stories.

On some teams, the London developers were happy to work on Bangalore timings. Although it meant that they needed to wake up by 5 AM, they were happy to do so because it gave them an opportunity to work from home for the rest of the day. The Bangalore team followed suit and occasionally worked during London hours as long as they were able to work from home. This was not mandated. The teams figured out their level of convenience while working together. This had an unexpected benefit. Because the folks in London were waking up so early to work, the Bangalore team owed it to them to do the same and ensured that pairing times were respected. Meetings were rescheduled, breaks were minimized, and even lunch hours were kept to a minimum out of respect for the early hours the Londoners were giving. In fact, the velocity for some projects was much higher than that of regular projects.

Tools

Tools are important. They enable interactions. They are catalysts for progress. But if a tool gets in the way of interactions between individuals, an alternative is needed. Our first project involving remote pairing pushed us to experiment with different tools. We tried several tools, including WebEx, GoToMeeting, join.me, and Chrome Remote Desktop. After many attempts, we identified that TeamViewer works best for remote pairing based on the developer inputs, even if it was the most expensive option. For audio, we found both Skype and Google Hangouts useful. Google Hangouts had the added advantage that up to ten people could be added for a discussion. When a team is going through such a sensitive engagement, the last thing anyone wants is for the folks to feel jaded due to communication hassles.

Developers are not used to being on calls for six to seven hours at a stretch. When we started off, our developers started using their personal headsets, but we soon realized that it was becoming stressful. After long hours, ears started to itch and ache. We found that Circumaural[1] headsets were the best tools to aid remote communication. Again, we chose the highest quality product. A couple of hundred dollars invested will be more than made up by increased velocity and sheer team enthusiasm.

These are Agile decisions. Our project budget did not specifically list the Circumaural headsets or the TeamViewer license costs. Strictly from a product perspective, these are peripheral requirements. Traditional project management would never have provided for these tools. In my prior experiences, the organization culture was such that team members would not even consider asking for better headsets. In many service organizations, especially offshore-based setups, maintaining a strict budget is given ludicrously high importance. I have been in situations where the

---

1. http://www.learningaboutelectronics.com/Articles/What-are-circumaural-headphones

developers' machines had 2GB of RAM. Developers were expected to work within constraints, simply because everyone else was doing so. Even if the project leaders wanted to reverse the situation, organizational norms got in the way. Sometimes, organization policy will allow project managers, but not developers, to have laptops. Often, the project manager's laptops were more powerful than the developer's workstations.

I have also encountered situations where the client does not want offshore developers using laptops for fear of customer IP going outside the secure zone. Onsite developers are usually provided far greater access. These types of arrangements are quite anti-Agile. Given how far technology has progressed, you can no longer create IP security through physical lock-downs. A majority of developers have smartphones that are always connected to the Internet. These discriminatory setups are also blatant obstacles to developing an ownership mindset.

Our stand-up meetings usually used Google Hangouts. We created a Google group for the team to use and had each member of the team join. To be honest, not everyone joined every time, but it was our daily catch-up. Under the circumstances, it worked pretty well. That is what being Agile is about: evolving on the situation as it emerges, making the best use of the situation and the resources available, but at no point compromising on the end objective.

Be Agile and Build Ownership

We used Agile principles heavily to ensure that we were on the right track. In every iteration, we created a story relevant to the ownership transfer. At the end of the iteration, the developers who were taking over relayed what skills or capabilities they had picked up with respect to that component. At that point, we considered the story closed. The focus was not on knowledge. It centered around what points the developers had become confident with. Some typical questions were

- Are you confident you can fix a regression issue that comes around this area?
- Are you comfortable with fixing a production defect that comes in this area?

It can be difficult to give a "yes" or "no" answer to these types of questions. The emergence of defects and issues can be unpredictable. Some high-severity defects can be easily fixed and some low-severity defects can be highly frustrating to resolve. It is natural for developers to feel they do not know everything about the system. Some may say, "We know what we've worked on. But we don't know if this is all there is to it, or if there is something else that we don't know about."

Therein lies the art of ownership. No one would ever claim to know everything. We all work on subjective and relative grounds. There will always be someone who knows more about a system than others. These are the folks who become subject matter experts. Over time, by working on a system, people cultivate expertise. That should not come in the way of taking ownership. Ownership is about being responsible.

The slogan for Fortis Hospitals Gynecology Center is, "Where mothers are born." It is quite profound. How many first-time mothers are experts in childcare? None. "Mothers" are born at the same time their babies are born. They all learn along the way. In an ideal world, no parent would give their baby to someone and say, "I don't know how to care for her, so please take her away from me." Parental instinct will take over, evolve as the bond between her and her child grows, and create ownership. When the parent realizes there is something that they don't know, they consult elders, medical practitioners, and other experts in childrearing. At the same time, every baby is raised differently. Depending on the home environment, the means, the situation, and a host of other factors, babies go through different experiences and are instilled with different values. No one is expected to know everything when a child is first born. Childrearing is, in its purest form, taking ownership of the raising of a child.

Similarly, the developers taking over the project in the earlier set-up were also less informed about the system. Indeed, several areas of the application had not been touched in years. The folks who had developed those modules were not around anymore, but that did not stop the previous teams from taking ownership. The same holds true for the new setup as well. At the same time, it is very important to provide a level of assurance to the new teams. For this purpose, we ensured that some level of expertise was available in Bangalore as a support system for the London developers if they faced challenges along the way. We did not put a time limit on the support. It was a wait-and-watch mode. However, the Bangalore developers were not sitting idle. They continued to work on other components and deliver value to the business.

As mentioned earlier, the London developers were asked about their confidence in supporting modules they are taking over when in production. This questioning forces the team to think beyond the immediate story that they are playing. At a subconscious level, expectations are set for what ownership really means. It makes a tremendous difference in learning. The type of questions addressed become vastly different. Learning then gets focused on sustenance as well and not just enhancement.

Code Comfort: Working Code over Documentation

What is working code? It's not just the software enabling the feature to work in production. It's the sum total of the application code, the automated test cases, and the build deployment scripts that ensure the right versions of the application can be tested and taken live. Working code begins with testable code. Working code is the soul of the application. No amount of diagrams and documentation can make up for working code. When you create a document, you are also creating an expectation to maintain that document. Ensuring that the document is up-to-date with the code can be difficult. Any developer will look for code comfort rather than what is written about the code. Hence, the primary focus ought to be on remote pairing and delivering features. The secondary objective would be to develop knowledge about the code base. Automation tests are an intrinsic aspect of software development. One of the best ways for developers to understand functionality is to run through tests. Tests are an excellent way to appreciate the functional expectations from the application. Because our program at EuroT had followed test-driven development (TDD)[2], it aided in the ownership transfer as well.

I believe the concept of code comfort is a fundamental pivot on the traditional expectations around documentation. Documentation in software development has long been glorified as the only means to transfer knowledge. In the Agile world, we seek code comfort rather than documentation comfort. Our developers did not spend time going over high-level and low-level designs. Where something was not clear, developers used the pairing tool and did a pencil sketch of the module in question. This usually comes naturally to developers when explaining something. If the drawing made sense to be saved and shared, it was put into the work space where all the files were saved.

I do not mean to deride documentation or the need for it, but we have come to a state where documentation has become an objective in itself. In previous projects, I have been part of reviews where developers have been castigated because they are poor at documentation. In these cases, we unfortunately create an anti-pattern. Team members begin to focus more on how to document instead of actually writing code and communicating about it. At the same time, we do not allow for effort to develop the documentation. In my previous role of project manager, when I coached the team to add points for documentation, the client management rejected it.

Communication is key. Documentation is an aid to communication. At EuroT, one of the units to be transferred over was the architecture of the platform—not at the module or functionality level, but abstracted at a much higher level. This required some medium for us to articulate. There is really no code, as such, for architecture. Architecture is how the system has been envisaged. In this case, we created a couple of diagrams, but we also recorded a walkthrough of it using the diagram as a medium. This video was then uploaded onto the document repository system along with the diagram itself. Using both documentation and a video allowed us to communicate more effectively.

---

2. www.agiledata.org/essays/tdd.html

The trouble with documentation is that it does not convey the emotions, history, and a lot of the unstated knowledge that has gone behind making the system what it is. It especially doesn't convey the questions around architecture. Senior developers will usually be more interested in the "why" than the "what" and "how." Given experience and skill sets, the "whats" and "hows" are easy to acquire. What raises questions is why something has been designed in a certain way and why a different method was not adopted. A lot of decisions made over time may look silly years later. After all, systems and technologies advance at a rapid pace. For various reasons, our platform may not keep pace with evolution. Articulating all of this on paper is impossible. A walkthrough will only take you so far. The person who has lived the experience can tell a story. Capturing it on video helps pass on some elements of that story through an audiovisual medium. Ownership transfer involves transferring history, context, and thoughts as well as commitments.

The Product Principle

Who is the customer for an ownership transfer program? At the lowest level, the team taking over is the customer of the team handing over. One level higher and the customer can be defined as the business and functional teams for whom the entire IT organization is a service provider. Go up another level and it becomes the corporate customers and end users of the application to whom the entire organization is beholden. As we move towards higher planes of service and customer definition, we realize that the people on those planes are much removed from the action. The end user would likely not even be aware that an ownership transfer program is underway. In fact, the end user might not even care. All she would expect is that the application is fast, easy to use, and reliable. Ultimately, she is the end customer for the program. In a sense, ensuring the satisfaction of that end user is also the purpose of the product transfer.

Sometimes we lose this perspective in the daily grind. Members from every unit in the organization are in some way responsible for making the program a success. That is the starting point for collaboration. In some ways, we as developers are responsible to that end user. That makes it incumbent for everyone within the organization to be aware about the program. Most transfer programs will have the CIO as the sponsor. In our case, the CEO had a keen eye on the program. After all, one of the prime purposes of the program was to bring down capital expenditure.

Service-level agreements and penalties seen in today's contracts abet practices that are self-rewarding but purpose-defeating. Negotiating on such clauses can take us further away from serving the true needs of the end customer. Discussions centered on time needed to fix faults and system availability make it sound as if these are negotiable parameters when, in fact, the digitally enabled end user expects the system to be always available with no faults. Today, true customer needs center around differentiated service and an engaging user experience. These call for a product mindset, but that mindset cannot be driven through contracts.

Establishing the right working relationship and pledging to a common cause are far more crucial than going over the minutiae of the contract clauses. The customer organization has a much bigger role to play in this case. The CIO and senior IT leaders will need to work extra hard to bring in the right levels of sobriety and cooperation to the engagement. Contracts should only be a necessary evil for organizations to engage. They are best left for the legal team to iron out.

On Change

In earlier sections, I referred to the sophisticated plan we had come up with for the EuroT transfer: a plan that looked good on paper. By the time we concluded the exercise, the original plan had been completely overhauled. The plan evolved as we moved forward. Several things came off the priority list, and several new things were added. Out of the 17 units we had identified, we managed to transfer over only ten of the original units and a few new items that had come up. Our division of the original units ended up getting redone. At one point, we had thought that Bangalore would be down to ten members and London would have added about 15 additional members. At the end of the project, there were 20 members in Bangalore and London had not expanded as much as originally expected. But the spirit, direction, and the momentum embodied in the original plan was carried forward. The EuroT CEO, William Henderson, declared the program to be a resounding success.

One of the cardinal Agile principles is to set priorities and the expectation with stakeholders that only 70 percent of what is planned will get transferred over. The ten units mentioned earlier did encompass more than 70 percent of what was originally slated to be transferred. Why is this important? For a program such as the EuroT project, you can never get all the requirements right the first time. The incumbent will know the subject matter, but they do not know how much the target team already knows. The new team could be well aware of some elements you might not expect. For example, if the new team was already comfortable with the technology stack, some of the effort could be less than anticipated. Or if the team is not comfortable with the build and deployment process used in the program, more time may be spent discussing those, which ends up increasing effort on the transfer. The incumbent may assume certain aspects around process as a given and then realize that the entire approach of enhancing and maintaining a module will change with the handover. Or, you may find that the target team is very comfortable with the domain and functionality, which speeds up the transfer process.

Some handovers, such as release processes, may actually be to a team who are already experts in the process. So all of that may be accomplished is handing over the module, which the release team then absorbs into their scheme of release activities. The release team's approach to the task may also be quite different from those of development teams. In this case, the initial discussions could span a longer period of time because the forming, norming phase can be disproportionately high.[3]

In the Nerup program described earlier, what started off as a transition plus delivery exercise changed completely, with Areker Bank choosing to retain both the Sofa Engineers and LeanAgile engineers. The program became a full-fledged delivery program. Sofa Engineers had superior product knowledge, but their system integration and delivery skills were not proven. Areker Bank was trying to address the delivery challenges and began with the idea of a complete transition to LeanAgile. However, as the project progressed, it moved to a point where both the LeanAgile teams and the Sofa Engineers worked side by side to deliver a major release. Discussions continued for eventual handover for support and maintenance, but the focus on transition was completely altered.

The triple constraints of a project are scope, cost, and time. Adept project managers have a firm understanding of which is the most rigid constraint and which is the most flexible. In Agile projects, timeline and cost are typically rigid, whereas scope is the most flexible. This is often true in ownership transfer as well. In this case, scope could be defined as transferring ownership for specific elements on the product. Change is inevitable. Embracing change is the best way to approach dynamic programs such as these.

Things to Know and Do

- Focusing on interaction and collaboration between people is critical. Identify and procure tools and processes based on requests from the team on the ground.

- Agile principles can be a great way to build ownership. Create stories that track ownership transfer over iterations.

- Create a sense of code comfort for the new team. The team should be comfortable fixing issues when they arise. That can be achieved only by working on the code and not by going over documents.

---

3. www.mindtools.com/pages/article/newLDR_86.htm

- The North Star for all teams should be a healthy product, which translates to a satisfied customer. This over-arching principle will enable teams to resolve mutual conflicts and work to a common goal.

- Be ready to evolve the program plan as you move into execution. As more details are understood, the need to evolve the plan further becomes clearer.

Chapter 6

Culture

The word *culture* has its origins in Roman times from Cicero, who coined the term *cultura animi*, or "cultivation of the soul."[1] As it was redefined in the 20th Century by anthropologists, *culture* has come to mean the ideas, customs, and social behaviors of a particular group of people. When two groups of people meet over any intense social activity, there will be fireworks. Think back to any wedding you have attended. While it's a moment of celebration for those attending, it almost seems like an ordeal for those organizing. People from different walks of life, distinct beliefs and life stories come together to create an orchestra of dramatic proportions.

A transfer program is first and foremost a social activity. Two teams from different organizations, regions, and backgrounds come together to execute this delicate dance of give and take. National culture is stronger than organizational culture. This has been studied and proven across different multinational companies.[2,3] This must be noted by the leadership, especially during times of ownership transfer that involve personnel from different nationalities. Bridging the national cultures is effort-intensive even when the transfer occurs between two groups within the same organization. This has become a routine activity for many multinational companies who have captive centers in different nations.

Every organization strives to create a unique culture that attracts and retains employees. A start-up, for example, typically has an informal culture with a

---

1. https://www.boundless.com/sociology/textbooks/boundless-sociology-textbook/culture-3/culture-and-adaptation-31/the-origins-of-culture-199-3031/

2. www.ukessays.com/essays/commerce/the-theoretical-studies-of-organizational-culture-commerce-essay.php

3. Adler, Nancy, *International Dimensions of Organizational Behavior* (Mason, Ohio: Thomson South-Western, 1983).

let's-get-it-done attitude. A large conglomerate will be far more bureaucratic; decision-making goes through several workflows. In large organizations, the attention given to legal ramifications and security constraints is much higher. As organizations get older, their risk-taking appetite tends to go down.

Power Distance

Well-known author and professor of Organisational Anthropoly and International Management, Geerte Hofstede came up with a framework for cross-cultural communication. One of the indicators in this framework was called *power distance*. This is a measure of how much the less powerful members in an organization accept and expect inequality in power. People in high power distance cultures are more deferential to their superiors. Individuals in low power distance cultures are more open to questioning authority and are keen to participate in decisions that affect them. Power distance is also heavily determined by organizational culture. However, high power distance can sometimes have catastrophic consequences. For example, Korean Air Flight 801 crashed on August 1997.[4] The captain decided to attempt a visual landing, without the use of radar equipment. He had landed on that air strip several times before so he was confident he could do it. However, on that fateful day, the weather was terrible. His crew realized the danger and tried to warn the captain. The flight engineer asked the captain, "The flight radar has helped us a lot?" What he was really saying was "don't land manually." The captain responded, "Yes. They are very useful." None of the crewmembers took control of the flight out of deference to the captain, and 223 people died on that fateful flight.

Cross-Organizational Cultures

Service organizations that typically form the vendor segment in a transfer exercise can have different cultures, and these can affect the cultures of their clients. An up-and-coming service organization, for example, will be far more flexible to their vendor's requirements. This often translates into the organization's members melding seamlessly into the client culture, causing fewer cultural conflicts within teams. In other words, the customer culture significantly surpasses the vendor culture. However, in the case of large organizations such as IBM and Accenture, the equations are different. These service organizations are giants and their organization culture will reflect this in their engagements. These translate to interesting dynamics at the team level.

---

4. National Transportation Safety Board 2000. Controlled Flight Into Terrain, Korean Air Flight 801.

When Vendor Culture Blocks Organizational Progress

Triborg, a large Fortune 50 company, had partnered with a big IT organization, Pinstripes. Over time, the composition of the teams within Triborg's IT centers shifted. Three out of five members in each team were from Pinstripes. Pinstripes' relative weight in decision-making increased. A project's milestones, release schedules, and scope were decided based on Pinstripes' bandwidth, capacity constraints, and delivery processes. Triborg was acutely aware of their relative lethargy compared to their competition. They were forced to witness the evolution of continuous delivery from the sidelines even as their competition raced ahead. Any discussion about changing releases or processes were met with challenges from Pinstripes. Triborg finally decided to make substantial changes to their IT team structure. They hired more in-house team members and gradually realigned the balance between the client and vendor members.

Compared to other companies, the power distance within ThoughtWorks is quite small. ThoughtWorks follows a very flat structure with no hierarchy of any sort. The company has always followed a model of servant leadership. As employees, then, we are used to endless debates and discussions before decisions are made. Quite often, decision-making would be more of an evolution as opposed to a final decision. Most of our clients, on the other hand, have a more traditional structure with fairly straight hierarchies within teams. Among our clients, teams generally tend to agree with the opinion of the managers. In a similar vein, client managers expect decision-making to occur over meetings with their counterparts from ThoughtWorks.

Greater Power Distance in Conflict with Agile

CentOS is a large organization with a captive center in India. It is also extremely hierarchical. Managers are accountable to their bosses for delivery, which makes work prioritization largely a matter of keeping the boss satisfied. In fact, managers regularly refer to their superiors as "boss" and "big boss." Negotiations on regular prioritization get completed quickly. The common refrain is, "Boss wants to see it tomorrow." The boss often changes what gets done within a sprint without necessarily appreciating changing priorities

(continued)

within a sprint can have a negative impact. The boss merely feels entitled to see a story played immediately and uses his position to decide what becomes priority. In another instance, the team is asked to do a demo specifically for the senior manager. The manager has requested this demo, as she was otherwise busy in important meetings that were considered a higher priority.

In this organization, accountability has been well established. Each person is accountable to his supervisor for the work getting done. This has begun to supersede what is good for the project. Ownership gets diluted because each member is looking for his superiors to handle the decisions on what the priority is on their projects. Their job is merely to execute those decisions.

The following examples take a deeper look at the impact of culture in the daily practices of the ThoughtWorks and EuroT teams. These examples of the working style differences between teams should resonate with most enterprises.

Team Culture and Process

It is important to differentiate culture from process. Culture has deep impact on decision-making. What seems an obvious decision to one group could be anathema to another. In the case of EuroT, both locations followed similar Agile practices. They each had stand-ups, iteration kick-off meetings, and retrospectives. However, what happened within these events differed dramatically across locations. Take the case of the stand-up itself. At one time, the size of our team in Bangalore had become rather large. This was necessary because we were going through the process of ramp-downs. As we ramped-down, we also had to merge teams, eventually decreasing from four teams to one. Over the following months, the team would continue to decrease from 25 members to 10. We made a conscious decision to keep it as a single team as we ramped down. During that time, we also wanted to ensure that the stand-ups were not going out of control. So we did a "walk the wall" rather than have every member give an update. The "walk the wall" approach focuses more on the stories and defects in play as opposed to every member giving an update. Because we were using the concept of pairing, it brought down the number of updates virtually by half but without losing the core principle of the stand-up. A prime driver on this was to keep stand-ups brief and to the point. This idea came from the team members themselves. The culture in Bangalore ensured open communication and we were able to change how stand-ups are run.

For one of the teams in London, on the other hand, stand-ups followed a task-based approach. In a sense, this meant the stand-up was more detail-oriented. Pair switches did not occur as much in London. Developers tended to become specialized in specific areas. The same developers usually picked up stories in the same areas.

In London, the teams also followed a model of taking a vote of confidence as part of their stand-ups. This was a simple gesture: a "thumbs-up" or a "thumbs-down." "Thumbs-up" meant that you were confident of completing all tasks in the iteration. "Thumbs-down" meant otherwise. As can be expected, at the beginning of the iteration, all team members gave a "thumbs-up." As the iteration progressed, a few changed their position to "thumbs-down." By the last day of the iteration, if we had not finished all stories, everyone would give a "thumbs-down."

Large takeovers involve multiple teams. Each of these teams bring out their own unique cultures. The level of openness and the general disposition to engage in transitions differs from team to team. It is no wonder, then, that some transitions go rather smoothly whereas others don't, even within the same program.

Another cultural difference attributable to geography is the practice of frequent huddles.[5] In Bangalore, we used huddles when someone was stuck with a problem. Typically, huddles were focused on the technical side. When someone was not able to move ahead with a particular story, or was confused about which approach to take, they would call a huddle. If there was a lack of clarity about requirements, they would ask the business analyst (BA). However, given that the commercial teams were stationed in London, it would take some time to get clarity on requirements, longer than it would normally take with a huddle.

Huddles occurred frequently in London as well, but the big difference was the coverage on the huddle. Given the business, infrastructure, and business teams were all housed in the same office, one could huddle in these teams as well as any other relevant stakeholder. London had put a structure in place wherein IT teams started to sit in along with the business teams. This proximity created easy access among the teams, as well as familiarity with one another. Teams started working in a true spirit of collaboration after the imaginary and physical walls had broken down. This also meant that leverage and level of negotiation were far greater than in Bangalore.

The level of detail in stories was different between Bangalore and London as well. In London, the practice was for the developer to call a huddle before the start of any story. The huddle involved the developer, the BA, and the QA. They would discuss what ought to occur on the story then move forward with their work. This practice was not followed in Bangalore. Stories were analyzed to a finer level of

---

5. Team meetings called by any team member to discuss a blocker or a technical issue.

detail in Bangalore. This was partially because Bangalore was located farther from the business's end user. The BA had to get a fairly detailed level of understanding of the story and relay it back to the team in Bangalore. In Bangalore, the BA had the responsibility of a proxy end user for the developers, literally thinking like the actual product owner. This level of understanding was written down and agreed on between both parties. The by-product was that requirements were documented to a higher level of detail.

Retrospective Culture

The concept of retrospectives is crucial for Agile projects. The recommendation is that every iteration is followed up with a retrospective (or *retro* for short). London followed this recommendation to the hilt. The first day of a new iteration would start with a retrospective in the morning and the iteration planning meeting in the afternoon. A lot of smart practices had evolved within the retro itself. As the iteration progressed, the team members wrote up the points they wanted to discuss on cards and stuck it up on the team wall. As the iteration progressed, everyone could see what issues were coming up that needed to be discussed. On the morning of the retro, people knew ahead of time which points would be discussed.

People sometimes used novel methods to convey their sense of the way the iteration had panned out. In one retro, folks had to draw a picture that would convey their emotions. They would then need to explain what their drawing meant to the rest of the team and explain why they felt that way. Another method was to stand closer to the table if they were happier. Those who were not that happy stayed a little behind. Although these practices were seemingly quirky, they helped to create a relaxed environment in which people could discuss things without fear or favor.

In London, a retro started by picking up the action items from the previous one. The owner of the action item had to give a status update. If the action item had not been worked upon, the owner had to explain why. Afterwards, the meeting proceeded with the retrospective discussion. Teams made active participation all through the retrospectives.

In Bangalore, retrospectives did not occur frequently. Because we were not working on the action items, the interest in the retro itself waned. Retros were triggered only if an event of significant proportions emerged. The retros that did occur in Bangalore often started off with the team identifying issues to be discussed and then moving into the discussion. This meant that the time available for active discussion decreased substantially. Action items from the retros were captured, but they were not often followed upon later.

Iteration Planning Culture

Teams also conducted iteration planning meetings differently. In Bangalore, the business analyst did a team walk-through of the stories to be executed for the iteration and the teams discussed the implementation details. Subsequently, the team suggested points for the story based on planning poker,[6] a technique used by Agile teams for estimations. When there were outliers, the team members tried to find common ground. Some of these discussions closed out quickly; a few became raucous. Developers have a tendency to get passionate about points of view. If things got out of hand, one of the team members tried to find a resolution. The resolution for the debate ranged from doing a spike, going back to the business to get further details or simple validations of key assumptions. Members volunteered to take action items out of these resolutions to help move things along. A high level of participation and a free, accepting environment was a defining feature of our organization. The unstated tenet at ThoughtWorks is, "involving everyone is more important than being decisive."

In London, meetings followed a different model. Story points did not get decided as often based on planning poker. Some teams size stories in days (as against points) during the iteration planning meeting (IPM). The BA does not lead the IPM. Instead, a lead developer, along with the BA, leads the IPM. In London, IPMs begin with fewer preparations; the discussions center more around prioritizing the feature to play first and identify which defects need to be addressed. Stories are looked at and tasks identified accordingly. As mentioned earlier, a separate huddle also occurs between the developer, BA, and the QA before the story is kicked-off for development. Requirements change regularly on stories in London as well. Hence, the initial estimates tended to change substantially in London.

How Distance Impacts Culture

Service lines focus on delivery efficiency. Product lines focus on product effectiveness. Teams closer to business worry lesser about the length of a story or feature and more about the criticality of the features going live. Staying close to the business groups enables IT teams to develop a product mindset. Opportunities to have quick huddles with the product owner and the project sponsor can radically change approaches and the priorities on stories. Teams positioned with the business groups have this advantage. Working out of Bangalore often gave our teams a service

---

6. https://www.mountaingoatsoftware.com/agile/planning-poker

orientation. This meant that those teams broke down stories to finer details, obtained virtual sign-offs from the product owner, and ensured timelines and story points were met.

One of our developers who traveled to London unexpectedly experienced the difference between these two different focuses. In Bangalore, we rigorously tracked story points and the completion of stories. In Bangalore, we felt much more bound to the cost and the timelines of the project. The distance from the business group created a service-oriented mindset in Bangalore, making the team feel more accountable for the time and effort spent on stories. If there were changes, we spoke with the business owner and explained what has changed. In London, changes in timelines and requirements were not considered as much of a problem. Their closer proximity to business created a level of comfort. As our developer continued with the story he had traveled to London to work on, he got more and more nervous. The story attracted new scope and kept changing even during development. It was only a while later he realized that "no one really cares about the number of days." Although this idea may well be facetious, it shows in stark contrast the effect of work culture.

Capacity and Culture

In London, available capacity was determined based on how many stories were pending from the previous iterations and on the number of people who had vacation plans. What capacity becomes available is then distributed for the new feature and defects. In Bangalore, capacity was not reduced for the next iteration because of ongoing projects. Our intent was always to ensure that what was picked up got delivered. Because we had been working on the system for such a long time, the velocity of our teams had been predefined over a period of time. Therefore, the capacity for the team was well known. It was expected that the team would throw out the correct points for any stories picked up. Two levels of sizing used to occur in Bangalore. The first one occurred at the end of the inception. The development pair would identify what was called the "planning estimate" for story sizes. During the IPM, the entire team took another look at the stories and gave another estimate. This was known as the "development estimate," and it was expected that the team would stay true to this story size. Therefore, even if there was hangover, we did not pick up a lesser number of stories. This proved very inconvenient in Bangalore because of the service-line mindset. However, the Bangalore management felt it was important to ensure that the metrics of the points delivered were consistent. Also, with the team removed from the business users, productivity and efficiency were the only variables they could control.

Culture and Ownership

Culture can also affect a team's ability to take ownership for the program. When members from different groups come together and partake in combined activities, daily practices begin to scratch at the veneer of team play. Distributed members in the team will start feeling isolated, out of sync and eventually disinterested. Senior management needs to intervene and ensure there is a strong sense of appreciation amongst team members, so as to keep individuals involved and engaged. The larger purpose can be lost amidst the tactical frictions of daily activities. Team norming is most important in this backdrop.

After several rounds of discussions, the leadership decided that although the original seeds of the plan were laid out in Bangalore, the London team ought to drive the program. London's uptake on commitment took a bit of time. After London finally picked up ownership for the transfer, a subtle but profound change occurred to the way the program was being run: It became a pull more than a push. In a sense, London became the consumer for the program and Bangalore the supplier. Bangalore developers became a part of the London team.

We had one team, which started off with remote pairing. The module being transferred was not completely new to the London team. They had some prior knowledge and were picking up the rest of the functionalities around it. However, we had not done an adequate norming session among these two teams, which created an undercurrent of negative emotions. Members were reluctant participants on the remote pairing, and this manifested itself in various ways. The Bangalore view was that we were just waiting on London to be able to assist them. London folks had their set of activities and when required pinged the Bangalore team. Synchronizing work schedules became a challenge. Bangalore staff had to stay late. Folks in London were not finding enough value through pairing. Team stand-ups became reluctant affairs. Each side had a different story to tell. After the first iteration, the team called for a retrospective. The time of the retro was set late in the evening for Bangalore and the two members from Bangalore chose not to attend. The next day, the London Development manager informed us that we don't need remote pairing anymore and that the London team could handle the module on its own. The leadership team in Bangalore became quite concerned. Was this because the members did not attend the retro? Was something not working out for a while and the retro incident became the last straw? Many thoughts went through our minds. That entire morning we spent discussing and second-guessing what had happened. That afternoon, we received clarification that London wanted to pick up more responsibilities and learn more, even if they made mistakes. They felt that the mistakes would help them learn more. This was a slightly risky proposition, but given they wanted to take up ownership immediately, it was completely their decision to move ahead with it. From that point on, the London team took complete responsibility for the module.

Or so it seemed. The team had not accounted for the more than seventy defects logged against that module. Only about fifteen or so were of high severity. The others were lower severity defects that had existed for a long time and would likely never get addressed. The cost of fixing them was higher than the benefit fixing them accrued. But the process of moving them out of the bug tracking tool without fixing was not easy. Most organizations have their own labyrinthine protocols and bureaucracies. These twisted networks create communication overheads. This is one reason why any long-standing system has a large number of low severity defects that never get fixed. Most program managers hope these defects will die a natural death, and sort of just fade from public memory. But when one is doing an ownership transfer, these tiny problems often make their presence felt. The new team would not want to take ownership of these issues. It was a perfectly acceptable proposition. This was a team that was taking on responsibilities in addition to the ones they already had. They did not want to be steeped with work that quite frankly added no value.

The defects led to a discussion in which some developers from London suggested that any defect originating from existing code would need to be fixed by the team in Bangalore. This, in effect, would obviate the ownership concept we were trying to instill. The operational issue was that a different team would be working on the same code base to fix regression issues. We agreed on a model where Bangalore would address the high severity defects that existed as of that date. Any new defect would be addressed by the London teams. We used the opportunity of this ownership transfer program and picked up the entire lot of low severity defects and spoke to the appropriate groups. Most of those defects got closed.

The Politics of Culture

As Triborg, Inc. was in the process of ending their partnership with Pinstripes, they were making upgrades to their payment and checkout systems in parallel. This was being handled by their internal teams. Post-development, the maintenance was to move to a team under a different director within Triborg. The new team as well as the incumbent team found every way possible to keep interactions at a minimum. The current development team's manager, Akash, had only been in the organization for eighteen months. The new team manager, Janice, had been in the organization for much longer. Janice was far more assured and demanding of what she expected.

Meeting invitations from Janice would include only one member from Akash's team: the person who was there to speak about the specific module. Although there were team members from Janice's team seeded into the incumbent's, Akash went out of his way to avoid giving work to them. Interactions were awkward and guarded. Even when developers from both teams were pairing away, Akash kept tabs on the story, the discussions, and the outcomes. Both managers were deeply involved in managing the office dynamics.

Akash focused on completing development and moving on, but as is often the case with large, complicated systems, things were not working as expected. Some defects and performance issues still needed to be addressed. Janice's interventions were becoming more of an obstacle for him. When I suggested to him that we should look at the new team members as additional hands to resolve issues, his response was "Look, Vinod, we are trying to close shop here. We do not need additional hands and legs."

At that time, the big problem was application performance. Janice, though, had her own ideas of what her developers should work on and wanted her developers to focus on the security layer of the system. She understood that the security layer was the critical piece that needed attention. She wanted her tech lead to get up to speed within two weeks on the security layer. We argued that it would take him longer than two weeks and he should work on some pending defects and stories to get context. However, Janice had made up her mind and was sticking to her decision.

As expected, things did not transition smoothly. The only solution for management was to look again at the staff. Many of Akash's team members moved over to Janice's team. A couple of months later, Akash quit Triborg.

This situation could have been averted if Janice's and Akash's bosses had taken greater interest in the proceedings. They should have been involved early on and smoothed ruffles as the transition began to take shape. Their involvement came in quite late and occurred only after a significant portion of the budget was already used up. The only option in front of them was to reallocate staff members.

The EuroT transfer was not without its own issues related to office politics. One of the Bangalore developers had flown to London and was pairing with a London developer on the build systems. One of their activities as part of the engineering stream was to untangle services and make their builds independent. As can be expected, this process requires a level of discovery within the code. They would need to know how the build system was structured, what modules it impacted, which agents were driven by it and so forth. As they proceeded with the process and slowly untangled the code, a few build failures occurred.

However, what this pair realized soon was that every build failure was being attributed to them. There is often a tendency to blame the new kid for everything that goes wrong. Even when there were genuine functional issues causing build breaks, it was assumed that the build pair had broken it and they needed to fix it. The Bangalore developer found the experience quite challenging. She consistently needed to prove why a particular build failure was not due to her or her partner. Given the differences in culture and context, responding to the development managers demand for reasons for build failures was not easy to do. Many times, she felt it would have been easier to fix the build rather than to explain why the failure was someone else's fault. The EuroT CIO had called out this risk early on.

"Not Invented Here" Syndrome

The "not invented here" syndrome manifests heavily during transfer programs. Teams who are taking over will have a predisposition to ignore, negate, or completely reject the code developed earlier. This is a completely natural phenomenon. When we are faced with something different or contrary to our ideas, the first reaction is to reject it. This is perhaps the largest issue one would need to surmount on an ownership transfer exercise. It can manifest in many different ways. At the lowest level, the project environment will be tense. Many disagreements among project teams can be expected. At the highest level, you run the risk of needing to recreate the entire platform. The cost implications are huge. In between, you run a continuum of risks, starting from minor regression issues to debilitating production impacts.

The vendor's management can unintentionally foster this sentiment. One of a vendor manager's first activities is to identify the flaws in the system they are taking over. They can then take these points and use them to negotiate on contracts, SLAs, and penalties. However, the engineers perceive it as a message that finding fault is a good thing. In fact, it is more of a way to ensure that they don't take the blame for any problems.

This issue may show up during a transfer program in many ways. In the case of EuroT, we had several instances where the London developers derided the code and design. Over five years, the system had built up technical debt and, in isolation, the debt seemed unjustified. In these situations, you need to understand why these were created. Projects come with timelines and cost implications. Agile also professes that you must do as much as is required to generate business value in the quickest possible time. Having said that, you also need to keep the long-term implications of generating technical debt in mind. Making these calls are not easy. Inevitably, some technical debt will build up over time. In a sense, even low severity defects are functional debts created within the system. The EuroT leadership team noticed this issue and sent several messages indicating that the initiative was not to remove technical debt. This initiative was to take over the system, not to fix it. However, developers have a tendency to fix what is broken. That's why they are developers!

This particular issue created several difficult discussions. When folks in London questioned why a certain logic was built in a particular way or why a specific design pattern was used, the Bangalore developers would try to explain why the design made sense. London would not agree. As if in retaliation, Bangalore would then pick up another area of the code developed by London with potentially questionable quality and ask the same sort of questions they received regarding their code. Needless to say, this environment was charged with emotion.

When the "Not Invented Here" Mattered

In a different transition, the "not invented here" syndrome played out with a greater focus on functionality. I was part of an engagement in which a different team was taking over immediately after a product had been developed. This product was the personalization module of Varamele, Inc., a large organization with interests in retail, real estate, and home design. This Fortune 100 company was undergoing a technology overhaul. We were using the strangler approach to slowly replace the existing system.[a] Strangler trees start life in crevices on tree tops. Over time, these vines develop branches downwards while at the same time extending upwards to catch the sunlight. In the process, the host tree is strangled and may eventually die. Martin Fowler suggested that replacing legacy systems can be a process similar to the strangler vines. It made perfect sense to our current system replacement. The legacy system was already serving millions of customers and hence was critical to the business of the organization. We did not want to introduce disproportionate risk in trying to replace the application.

For various organizational reasons, one team developed the new user account management module while another team continued to maintain and enhance the existing module. As development neared completion, the legacy team came into the picture to take over ownership for the module. Given this team's domain appreciation and the type of customer situations they were accustomed to, they raised a number of functional gaps with the new application. The development team was working toward creating a minimum viable product (MVP), which could go live and be tested in production. The minimum viable product therefore drove certain design decisions to support an early release. The legacy team had a different understanding of what that

---

a. www.martinfowler.com/bliki/StranglerApplication.html

(continued)

minimum viable product ought to be. This was fundamentally driven by their own experiences and how they determined their priorities and stakeholders.

Based on this team's input, development went on for an additional three months, incorporating the minimum viable features as identified by the new team. In hindsight, it would have been better if the development team had been seeded with some members from the legacy team. However, the early focus was on technical skills and the Varamele management felt that a new team with the requisite technical skills would be the right way to go. At that point in time, they also felt the new team should not be "encumbered" with the old way of thinking. But when it came time for the rubber to hit the road, the older team proved its value. The relevance of domain understanding for ownership transfer is discussed further in Chapter 13, "The Three Bridges."

Culture in the Trenches—Pairing

In the case of EuroT, both locations followed a principle of pairing. However, there was a fundamental difference between ThoughtWorks and EuroT. ThoughtWorks is a service organization; their purpose is to provide IT solutions to their clients. ThoughtWorkers enjoy working in different setups. Our motivations are to broaden our perspective by working with different clients and on different technologies. Even within this program, ThoughtWorks had a fairly strong rotation policy. Most team members would spend about two years on a particular program and then move on to other projects. EuroT, on the other hand, is predominantly a product-based organization. Developers within the organization were not looking to move on and work with other customers. Their motivations were geared more toward obtaining deeper knowledge than a broad-based approach. When joining EuroT, they already were aware of what was in store. This was likely enough of a reason for London to already have adopted a product-first approach. These perspectives had profound impact on both the teams' approach to pairing.

For ThoughtWorks, pairing ensured knowledge-sharing which, in turn, ensured less dependency on specific individuals. Pairs changed once every two to three days, so a large story might be worked on by up to four to five developers. The interactions among these developers, with multiple sets of eyes looking at the code, ensured a level of natural code review. The overall quality of code increased. When it was time for a developer to roll-off, there would be fewer risks for the program because others within the group would also have enough context. But this came at the cost of reduced velocity. This also required an extremely strong set of automated test suites to catch issues ahead of time. You would continuously see "non-experts" in a domain working on stories.

In a product setup, it helps for developers to absorb knowledge and become subject-matter experts. This meant that the practice of pairing was diluted because one pair typically started and ended working on an entire story, even if it ran for a few weeks. Depending upon the situation, pairs sometimes broke up and worked on individual components within the story. This helped stories get done faster. They built context, and any issues concerning that feature were inevitably routed to this group. These developers would become indispensable to the organization. Because the subject-matter experts continuously worked on a single area, the number of potential defects was also less. Unfortunately, this can lead to creating anti-patterns such as going easy on the automation test scripts. We often observed that London's velocity was higher than Bangalore's. London did not have a practice of rolling off developers from an ongoing project. The downside to this method was that when an important issue came up on a particular module, we had to wait for the developer to come back from vacation so the issue can be picked up. Other developers either did not have the confidence or the interest to pick up that area of work.

Culture of Toil

Each organization brings its own special nuances on culture. One customer I worked with, Centos, Inc., had done away with business analysts altogether within their organization. Product owners were driving the requirements. In most cases, these members operated out of the U.S., despite the development team being based in India. There were also onsite technical team members who coordinated with business. The team spent long hours over calls both early in the morning and late into the night. In fact, the culture had been drilled-down in such a way that team members took pride on how much time they spent at work. Mornings in India would start before 9 AM. An hour of onsite calls later, work would commence in India. Late evenings and nights would finish up with a further handover call. Although this may look like a fail-safe way of working in a 24-7 environment, we never had the right members attending all meetings. People were always either double-booked or just plain tired. So, things were often repeated during meetings. Culturally, this became accepted. People felt entitled to the odd breaks in meetings because they had been working so hard and long.

Culture of Documentation

Given that Centos, Inc. was still in its Agile transformation infancy, there continued to be a huge push toward documentation. When things got out of hand, managers immediately put out a table of action items and set up the next meeting. But that document soon lost its relevance and a new document was created for a different set of problems—or worse, a different perspective to the same problem.

Recently, there was a huge struggle in stabilizing a test environment at Centos. The development team itself had spent more than two person-months of effort. On top of that, network, build, release, and hardware teams spent considerable time setting it up. Although some had advised allocating extra time for this activity, this advice was disregarded. As weeks turned into months, the management's inclination was to document these leanings in the local intranet. This was a cultural habit. Documentation and reports are often akin to comfort food. Our suggestion was to have a specific retro, so the leanings would be drawn out and absorbed within the collective conscious of the teams. After that, immediately set up another environment, one in which hardware had already been provisioned. Because there was momentum, these tasks would happen much quicker. It also offered an opportunity for the team to immediately apply what they had learned and to internalize this knowledge. However, the client was more interested to move on with the development activities which had been impacted given the effort on environment stabilization. Setting up the next environment would come back to haunt us in another four weeks and we would need to start all over, document or no document.

Ownership Is Taken

Arival systems had recently won a big prestigious order to handle a large application. Their customer was the IT organization of Creekside Corp, a Fortune 50 company manufacturing heavy machinery. This application had started off as a small set of scripts to handle raw material inputs into factories and had evolved over time. Creekside Corp grew into a large conglomerate with manufacturing bases in several countries. As a multi-billion-dollar organization, they were also split along various business lines. Their IT organization was equally complex. Different countries and business units had their own IT support groups. As the application proved to be useful for one group it was shared with the rest of the organization. However, in each case, tweaks were needed in the application to fit in with the various departments' business purposes. As time went by, several groups within the IT organization were running different versions of the application. Management eventually realized that this application had become critical but had also become unwieldy. There were many instances of production stalls as the application began to crash. No one had a complete understanding of how it worked. When people hit a snag, they would send off generic notifications hoping someone would have an answer. There were also frequent disputes among people who believed they were running the "correct version" of the application.

Creekside IT decided to centralize the application and hand over its maintenance to Arival systems. This was a prestigious win for Arival. They were not just taking over the maintenance of the application; they were centralizing the application and simultaneously supporting different manufacturing centers across nations and business groups.

This was also a huge challenge for the Arival team. None of the IT groups within Creekside really felt they owned the application. Every group said that it was really not their job to maintain this system, but they were doing it because business required them to. They would be happy to have the team at Arival take it off their hands. At the same time, every IT group's manager was keen to understand the rules of engagement between Arival and their manufacturing units. Every IT group wanted to be part of the lines of communication between Arival and the manufacturing units, but no one was prepared to spend time with Arival and tell them what they knew of the application.

Arival systems faced a unique challenge to take ownership for an orphaned application. They were also faced with the challenge of gleaning information from people who were not interested in helping. One way to address this was to place team members from Arival within the IT groups supporting the application. These team members would be tasked with learning about the application, supporting the business groups, and understanding further nuances within the application. This was tremendously challenging for the team members from a cultural standpoint. These types of situations require great support from the leadership team of the IT organization.

It was also important to define the problem at the right level. The purpose of the program was really to decrease factory downtimes. The ownership transfer was a means to that end. This higher order definition gave a larger purpose to the engagement. It also aided in passing the right message for Creekside Management to all stakeholders. It helped dissolve many walls of insecurity amongst the Creekside engineers.

Some things to consider when addressing these situations are:

- Do not tie down the contract with stringent timelines. You are entering uncharted waters. There should be opportunities to course-correct.

- Continuously evolve the to-be state as well. Centralization in this instance involves changes to the code, communication structure, maintenance processes, and enhancement models.

- Have regular checkpoints. You may find that centralization itself may not be such a good idea as you begin to understand some of the further challenges.

The Arival engineers were not made to feel welcome by the Creekside group IT engineers. The Creekside engineers were constantly busy with their work and did not give any time to assist the Arival engineers. The Arival engineers found themselves to be orphaned much like the application they were trying to adopt. There are no silver bullet answers for these situations. The new team members have to find ways to harmoniously meld with the current team.

However, the new team cannot do it by themselves. Like the iceberg principle, there is more beneath the surface. The softer issues and the accompanying politics involved drive the transition forward. All transitions have a push and a pull effect. The push elements are those that are driven from the top. The pull elements are those that evolve from the ground-up. In this case, the push factor had to take precedence, at least in the initial stages. The Creekside management needed to impress upon the incumbent engineers the need to spend time with the Arival engineers. In business parlance, they needed to "sell" the idea to Creekside engineers so they would cooperate. It always helps to discuss the problem and the solution from the point of view of the incumbent engineers. If the incumbents appreciate the value they derive from cooperating to hand over the application, they will be more forthcoming in their interactions. Some ways to motivate the engineers would be:

- Be transparent about the reason for the move. Provide numbers such as factory downtimes due to unstable applications and the associated costs need to be shared with the teams.

- Have an open discussion, attempting to understand and appreciate their concerns.

- Paint a picture of a future in which these engineers will no longer be held back and can focus on more interesting work.

- In this instance, there was little chance of anyone losing their job. The reductions in factory downtimes would more than support the Arival group's cost.

However, where situations of retrenchment exist, have an open discussion with the personnel. Reassure everyone that the transition will not occur within a short period of timed but over a longer duration. Levels of insecurity and hostility will decrease much more when people know they are not getting fired within a couple of months. If people were given a one-year horizon as an example, they would be far more forthcoming. In today's fast changing business world, getting a one-year assurance is often a luxury even under normal circumstances.

The Arival engineers had a huge task on their hand. As the application was taken over, the team would need to effect both engineering and process changes around the upkeep of the application. (These themes will be discussed in Chapter 7, "Engineering" and Chapter 11, "Process.") This is both a transfer and a transformation exercise, but there is little agility in the exercise. The Arival engineers began their work with stabilizing availability for the factories.

The common thread through all these incidents is that the team taking over ownership had a far higher degree of responsibility than the team giving it away. The new team will be the one to live with it. So it is in their interest that they understand every nuance of the application.

Pulling Them Together

Culture conflicts are to be expected in transitions. These are soft aspects that lie below the surface and like icebergs, undercurrents can push the elements below the surface and drive the entire program. There is no fool-proof way to resolve cultural issues. When a hammer is used on a nail, it produces good results. But if the same hammer is used on glass, the results are going to be drastically different. Similarly, what might be a solution in one organization may work completely differently in another organization.

That being said, the best approach to take in such instances is to understand the long-term goal. Eventually, there will be only one team—the one that is taking over. Therefore, it makes sense to let the new team decide what makes best sense for them. Align processes and practices to suit the new team's level of comfort. Having to make "compromises" does not come easy, but part of growing is knowing what works for us would not work for someone else. Motivations are different for different organizations. The trick is to strike that right balance between being actively involved and letting go of strong positions. It calls for a position of detached involvement, being actively involved with what is going on, but not interfere with the other person's story.

Groups within an organization cultivate their own cultures. Different development teams exhibit unique working styles and cultural differences amongst groups are amplified even further. The working styles of the IS teams, release teams, and the development teams can be vastly different. Involving all of these groups into an ownership transfer exercise requires significant investment in norming activities. Most ownership transfer exercises will result in changes to existing processes, working relationships, and organization structure. Structural changes are not always headline creators. Many changes are often subtle and merely redraw expectations.

In the case of EuroT, we had decided to unbundle the services as part of the transition process. Our purpose in unbundling the services was to enable discrete deployments into production. Although the development teams could work on unbundling the services without involving other groups, we eventually needed to involve them for release on demand. The IS and release teams are integral units for production deployments. Delaying these conversations only delays surfacing impediments for release on demand. The release and IS groups have unique perspectives and challenges to surmount when moving to a continuous delivery model. At the same time, these teams bring simple solutions to perceived challenges the development teams are facing.

One key success parameter for us at EuroT was that during the exercise we did not encounter large production issues. There were five releases going out during the timeframe of the exercise. Over these releases, there was only one production issue that could be directly attributed to the transfer program. The reason I bring this up here is because when we encounter disputes at tactical levels, it helps to step back and look for alignments from a broader spectrum. It is a major comfort when one knows that the entire organization is lined up to ensure tackling production issues. It often helps to start over from such points of convergence and then dig into issues causing divergence.

Things to Know and Do

- Culture plays a big role in the transition exercise. Cultural differences manifest across nations, organizations, as well as across teams.
- Cultural differences have the biggest impact in ownership transfer exercises. Like icebergs, 90 percent of the challenges lie beneath the surface. Managing these will require heavy involvement of senior management.

- Ownership has to be taken. The onus lies with the receiving team far more than the supplying team.

- Cultural conflict resolutions are highly nuanced. Unique solutions are required for unique situations.

- Keep in mind the long-term prerogative. Align cultures and practices to suit the new team's comforts.

Chapter 7

Engineering

Dosa, crepes, and pancakes—if you ask the connoisseurs, they will say they are vastly different products. If you ask the gastronomically advantaged, they would say these are from different regions or meant to be eaten at different times of the day. If you ask a child, she will say one is thin, one is fat, and one is in between. If you ask a hungry man, he will say they all are food.

Applications are like that as well. To the end user, it just serves a purpose. Whether I use Flipkart or Amazon is secondary to me. I am interested in purchasing a particular mobile phone. The site that helps me get it at the lowest price and the simplest manner is what I go with. I don't ponder on how the website is created, how the product availability is updated, or why there is a price difference. Of course, some users have preferences on the usability, the colors, the ease of navigation, and so forth. They are the connoisseurs of the Internet world. The rest have simple opinions such as "this website is useless" or "this website is cool."

But what is considered "cool" can change with the season. Our applications need to keep up with what users need. This is where engineering becomes essential. Engineering helps you to create outcomes consistently. It also allows for adaptation of procedures and tools to modify outcomes based on new demands. A properly engineered solution is not only durable, but also adaptable. In the case of software, engineering is not just about making the solution durable and adaptable. One also needs to engineer the factory that produces, maintains, and enhances the solution.

Transforming the Factory

In ownership transfers, you're not just transferring the application, but also the means to modify the application. The means is often overlooked when undertaking these exercises. The key here is the tools and processes used to make changes to the platform: elements such as how the application is tested, the process for continuous integration, and the way deployments occur.

At the same time, a disruptive activity like a transfer creates the opportunity to improve many things. At EuroT, five years of building and enhancing an application had created a monolith of sorts. The entire application was one large intertwined mass, with services entangled with each other and different pages calling different services and, of course, all of them dipping into a single data base. It was quite difficult to make changes to the application if you didn't have deep context and experience working on it. We had a fairly robust set of automated tests and that allowed us to make rapid changes, but any developer starting out on the program faced significant challenges to find her way around.

Adding one developer to a group of hundred members is one thing. You can still continue with the same monolith and have new people learn over time. But when you're transferring over the entire platform to a new group, such a large application will impose challenges. For EuroT, making improvements was not just a 'nice to have'. It became imperative. We had to entirely change the way things were run.

Our logical break-up of the platform into services helped out here. One of the first activities we took up was to separate the services: not just to untangle them, but also move them to be discrete, independently deployable components with their own repositories. This was quite important since the teams on the London side were structured as product-based teams. It meant that handing over a large system all at once would be counterproductive. Separating the services also eased ownership transfer between the two teams.

Automating Quality

Our services housed a lot of the business logic. Breaking these up was a compelling opportunity to transfer functional knowledge as well. Part of breaking up the services and making them discrete also meant we needed to provide quality assurance on the services independently. In the earlier set-up, automation tests were set up at a functional level. This meant that tests were run on the user interface (UI) layer, the web pages. Functionalities were automated so that a request would be transmitted from the UI layer through the services, to the database, and then back. But with the change of structure, the UI layer was separated from the services. Service tests needed to be created to vouch for the integrity of the services.

After business analysts, quality analysts best understand application functionalities. The reason is not hard to find. Test scripts are a great way to build functional knowledge. Service tests hence become an excellent way for upgrading one's functional skills. A system such as EuroT's uses heavy business logic. From the outside, there are only five pages to book a ticket, but the back end crunches several complex searches starting from the date and time of journey, the type of ticket, the number of travelers, and class of ticket in addition to the add-ons and mode of delivery. Writing service tests provide an excellent way to learn about the business logic of the system.

Versioning

Versioning is a critical component of software development. For a long time, the entire codebase of our platform had been versioned as a single system and deployed all at once. When the system was being built, there were vigorous additions to functionalities. It made sense to have the entire codebase as a single platform because almost all modules within the large system would get updated on a regular basis. Rather than spend time identifying which system had not been modified, it made sense to test the entire platform and put it into production. In the modifications, we used the concept of continuous integration. Whenever a developer checked in her code, the system automatically compiled the code, ran a set of "smoke tests,"[1] and provided an updated artifact set, including the entire codebase, with a new version number. The set of "smoke tests" are a representation of critical test scripts to ensure that the latest version will not fail spectacularly.

Over time, things changed. As the system grew larger, the number of changes became more localized to specific subsystems. The "smoke tests" started getting larger and larger. Every time someone checked in their code, it would take a long time before the "published artifact" would come out. At its worst, it took ninety minutes for the published artifact to come out. This was defeating the purpose of getting early feedback. The system began to resemble a lumbering elephant. This then started triggering anti-patterns. Developers were loath to check-in on time. No one checked in after Friday afternoon because if someone checked in and their check-in broke the build, it would take a long time to identify and fix the issue. Fixing the issue itself may not take time, but having to wait ninety minutes to make sure that everything was fine required more patience than most people had.

---

1. www.softwaretestingclass.com/smoke-testing/

Over time, a level of inefficiency had seeped into the system. We were not making regular changes to all subsystems, but we were still testing all subsystems. There was no other option because the entire code-base was a single block. It all had to be versioned, tested, and released at one go. What made sense for a smaller system was no longer practical. The entire cycle from start to release was now taking 11 weeks: six weeks of development and five weeks of system testing. Even small changes that everyone instinctively knew could go live sooner had to adhere to these 11-week cycles. Time-critical business changes had to wait because the cycle could only move at a certain pace. An 11-week cycle also made it difficult for developers. People would have made their changes and moved on to something else. Finding a defect or requesting a change nine to ten weeks after development slows down the developer. A developer will remember changes she made last week, but will likely forget changes made 11 weeks prior.

The above situation gave us a compelling reason to change the way things were engineered. We needed to break up the monolith into smaller subsystems. We also needed to change the system so that individual modules could be taken live at different times. This meant that the payment module could go live this week and the search functionality could go live three weeks later. To enable this, we needed to ensure version integrity was maintained. In short, this means that "version x+1" of the payment module needed to work seamlessly with "version x" of the search module.

Whereas service tests ensure the functional integrity within a module, integration tests will ensure that the functionality does not break across modules. This was essentially a second layer of safety net. While we brought in these testing elements, we also realized the need for team ownership. Every team had to abide by a "social contract" with other teams. Teams would have to inform other teams what worked or didn't work with the latest version and provide adequate information to other teams for them to be able to integrate their versions with the latest version. In addition, they were to take adequate responsibility to address any "technical debt" in their part of the code base. This means that they were responsible for cleaning up any issues with the code base that might result in performance-, security-, or deployment-related issues for the application as a whole.

Transformation through Ownership Transfer

Conventional transfer doesn't focus on engineering. In fact, the new team's management often uses the state of the code as a way to get service-level agreement (SLA) waivers. Lack of unit test coverage or not having the right build set-ups is used as a defensive tool by the new vendor to squeeze out SLA discounts. This becomes an "us versus them" attitude, which is in direct conflict with Agile philosophies.

IT organizations need to rethink the opportunities a transition provides for improving their engineering systems. Most organizations would agree that this area could do with enormous improvements. A new team can be more open and flexible in improving these areas. If organizations can sit down and have an honest discussion on this subject, many improvement initiatives would succeed as part of the transition.

Engineering has a direct link to quality and predictability. It's safe to assume that a transfer expects an improvement to quality and efficiency. At the very least, no one expects a dip in this area. Unfortunately, this aspect of ownership transfer situations is often overlooked.

Engineering activities are also very IT-centric. Most often, business groups will not appreciate the intricacies of software development, especially the ones pertaining to software engineering. Engineering improvements are akin to sharpening the saw before chopping. These activities are best timed to occur during transitions.

Every home is different. Although every loving household will provide an appropriate set of values, morals, and nourishment, how these are imparted will be different from home to home. When a child moves from one home to another, she will continue to learn and grow, but there may be drastic changes in how she is being reared. Some of those changes will be obvious, perhaps even dramatic. Some are subtle but profound. This can also be the case in how an application is built and enhanced. There is no one correct way to do it. But when an application changes hands, a lot of things change, including how one approaches its build and enhancements. In time, such engineering facets have a telling effect on how agile things will be. A move of this nature should bring more flexibility and adaptability.

Arival Story – The Engineering Dimension

As the Arival engineers began taking over the factory application from various groups, they were faced with the task of consolidating and setting it up as a single instance. They could not run many versions of the application to support all groups. As they began the process, they realized that not all Creekside factories required all features. In some instances, a feature of the application was contrary to another group's operations. The Arival group was caught in a bind. They had to reengineer the application (see Chapter 6, Ownership is Taken).

They decided to use a feature toggle concept so that they could toggle certain features on or off. The group set up configurations so that features could be switched on or off for specific factories. The group needed to take

(continued)

another look at the database and structures so each factory could be served without compromising on the integrity of other factory set-ups.

Operations were always running in some part of Creekside all the time. Arival realized they could not plan for downtimes on a centralized application at all. This created two additional requirements:

- Create abundant redundancy and availability for the system. Create a multisite approach for running the system. More on this in Chapter 8, "Infrastructure."

- Provide for an application release process with no downtimes for factories.

The applications did not have any automation tests. None of the Creekside teams had thought of implementing unit tests and automation scripts as they enhanced their applications. Because the application had grown so gradually, it hadn't seemed necessary. But during this time, this application was supporting dozens of factories across the world. Because it's difficult to manually test the application for every feature for every factory, the team had to identify and implement automation testing features of the application as well.

With the application becoming centralized, it needed to pick up additional features around Internationalization and multi-lingual support. Threat-modeling and security added a whole new dimension to the application. The Creekside engineers did not really have to think through their release strategy, but with centralization and a single team supporting different stakeholders, the Arival team had to put together and implement an elaborate branching and release strategy.

The engineering side of this transformation was equally challenging and involved as the ownership transfer. Both the transfer and the transformation need to be taken up together. Although the first priority for Arival would be to take over the applications, the group also needed to think about the end state.

Things to Know and Do

- Ownership transfer involves not just transferring the end product, but the factory set-up that produces the code and the means to change the application.

- Ownership transfer offers great opportunities to implement engineering changes to the application. Most often, there is also a transformation objective to the ownership transfer.

- Critical elements in engineering involve automation, continuous integration, and versioning of the application.

- Several nonfunctional aspects of the application such as security, response times, and even release cadence have a huge bearing on the engineering side of the application.

Chapter 8

Infrastructure

Ship the Shop

Just as you plan for bringing a new baby home from the hospital, when you take over an application, you also need to plan for the infrastructure and where it will be hosted. This is a very important, complicated element and something that often gets compromised. Think of it as someone shipping the whole shop to a new location without stopping the manufacturing. Now that can't be easy! When we talk of infrastructure, we don't mean just the production set-up. Infrastructure ranges from the development environment to the testing, staging, and finally, the production environments. Infrastructure can often end up being the costliest component of an ownership transfer exercise. Some instances of infrastructure may even require additional office space if a large number of people are joining the team.

There Is Software in Infrastructure, Too

Infrastructure involves not just the hardware, but also the software that drives the hardware. In today's world, most infrastructure runs on virtual machines. Each of these machines has its own set of operating systems and antivirus software. At EuroT, as the hardware moved from one location to another, we had a hard time keeping track of the software licenses that needed to go along with it.

Another aspect we focused on was automation. We had not automated many things around the infrastructure side in Bangalore. When this opportunity arose, we decided to automate as we transferred over the infrastructure. This was valuable for two reasons.

The first reason was in retaining knowledge of the transfer. We could have mapped each machine and manually cloned each virtual machine (VM) at London. However, manual errors could easily seep in. Validations typically take longer and are more complex on hardware. Therefore, we decided that automating the VMs would be our first step. Our process was to create the VM in Bangalore and run it in Bangalore. We got the opportunity to fine-tune the script to a level of stability. Then we used the same script and created a VM in London. We ran both VMs (Bangalore and London) simultaneously for a period of time. When we had obtained sufficient level of confidence, we shut off the Bangalore VM. In effect, we created knowledge on how to create specific VMs and those were made available as the automation scripts.

The second reason automation was valuable was to improve efficiencies as a whole. Automation of machine creation brings enormous benefits around both hardware optimization and machine maintenance. When we had releases, we needed to make configuration changes in as many as 24 different web servers. This used to occur manually. Mistakes were common and would get caught only during testing. So although there was no production impact, the process of configuration changes themselves was onerous and had to be performed with great discipline. The same procedure is far simpler after automation. Some of the tests were also automated. After the configuration script had been updated and tested, we could run the same script to upgrade all 24 servers. The amount of human intervention required became far less. The scope for mistakes also decreased. After a script has been created, it's far simpler to update it with configuration changes. It is certainly much easier to update a script as opposed to manually updating each machine. Because the script is version-controlled, it becomes much easier for people to see the changes made and who made them.

Engineering and Infrastructure

At EuroT, the changes around the engineering approach had a sizeable impact on what aspects of and how much of the infrastructure would change. As mentioned earlier, we decided to split the services as part of the transformation. This had an interesting consequence. Earlier, due to the large size of the application, each time a build was triggered, we needed more machines to power all of the services. After we had broken up the services, we could make do with running a slightly smaller set of services because the chances of something in "Y" service breaking due to a change made in "A" service was far less. This decreased the number of machines used in the build and deploy process, so we managed some optimizations on the hardware side.

The next important element for us was the transition of hardware across locations. The IT world often does not have the luxury of downtime in today's dynamic business environments. At EuroT, we could not switch off the application for any length of time. The only way forward was to run parallel systems in both London and Bangalore and ensure they run in sync. When we started the transition, the environment in Bangalore was stable and the environment in London was just being built. Even as we created the environment in London, we could not immediately bring down the Bangalore environment. The stability in London was still in question and could not be proved.

This meant that there was a period when the total number of machines running the application across both locations went up and peaked before coming down. Eventually the London team got comfortable with the new environment and we began switching off the Bangalore environments. The above incident showed that hardware requirements could actually go up before they decreased. Even in situations where the team sizes would shrink, this dynamic was a distinct reality. We also learned to plan for the maintenance of the additional hardware for a period of time and plan for the licenses required if we are running additional hardware. These elements are often not thought through before an ownership transfer.

Distributed Hardware

In the global spread of today's world, we often encounter situations where different teams across multiple locations are working on a single project. Several organizations are also making the transition to the cloud for their day-to-day operations.[1] In some cases, these moves are done in phases. The pre-production environments such as the development and testing environments are transitioned out to the cloud first. After the organization has a strong grip on the transition, the production setup also moves to the cloud.[2] This means that we regularly encounter situations where development and testing need to be occurring in two different sets of environments. The biggest challenge in such situations is to keep all environments in sync. In the case of EuroT, while both locations are working on the code and checking-in, it's very important to ensure that they are also synchronized.

This means that the version of code in Bangalore ought to mirror what is seen in London. If it doesn't, a smooth transition cannot occur. Application integrity is compromised and promoting to production is challenging. Having the applications automatically sync up across locations is crucial. This automated syncing calls

---

1. www.dummies.com/how-to/content/how-to-ease-the-transition-to-cloud-computing.html

2. http://bigthink.com/articles/how-to-transition-to-a-cloud-based-infrastructure

for additional investment and effort. The process of syncing, if done for the first time, can be a mini-project in itself with its own round of testing and fine-tuning. Our original plan at EuroT did not take into consideration the complexity involved in keeping two locations running in sync. In fact, the infrastructure move took up an additional million euros. These costs included additional hardware, software licenses, and additional team members from the IS teams. This additional investment paid for itself within a year as the capacity requirements lowered after the transition.

There were some devils in the details. Bangalore was using Symantec as its antivirus package, whereas London was using Sophos. When we were automating and transferring over, we could not test with Sophos in Bangalore. We had to move the automation script over without the antivirus package and then separately install Sophos in London.

Another thing to watch out for is license leakage. License leakage has to pay for license cost while not utilizing their value. When you create a VM, licenses are allocated to it, but you should also be equally careful to put the license back into the pool when destroying a VM.

The Infrastructure Team

In most organizations, the development teams are separate from the infrastructure (IS) teams. A completely different team and perhaps a different vendor may handle infrastructure. The infrastructure may be housed in a data center. All of this adds further complexities to operations. In the case of the EuroT project, we had not accounted for the challenges in coordinating and lining up schedules of the development and the infrastructure teams to enable these activities. Bringing in the IS teams was a bit of an afterthought. Because of this, they had to accommodate the transfer activities amid their already packed schedules.

The IS teams are always very close to the transition teams in the orbits of influence (refer to the "Orbits of Influence" section in Chapter 4). Most projects will require close coordination with the IS teams. Of late, compelling cases have been made for the DevOps model, in which the development and operations team are merged into a single unit. Several books have come out on this topic.[3] I tend to agree with the idea of merging the Development and Operations team into a single entity.

---

3. http://devops.com/2015/02/11/five-great-books-on-devops/

Challenges of Teams Working in Silos

Centos Inc, a large set-up with a captive facility in India, had streams of work running based on activities. They had one team for development, one for build and release, and another supporting the hardware. The many layers of orthogonal accountability created conflicts when these teams interacted with one another. Responsibilities are diffused as teams orient towards their group instead of the project. These teams focus more on their own activities and aim to maximize their utilization instead of working towards project outcomes.

Centos has been migrating its pre-production environments to a virtualized environment. This required some of the teams to learn Chef (a tool for automated infrastructure in the cloud). The build and release team was focused on setting up the cloud-based environment, but they never kept the development teams in the loop. When the build and release team was ready to migrate the applications to the new infrastructure, they faced severe headwinds from the development teams. The development teams were not pleased that their machines would need to be torn down and reset. The development team was used to making patch releases, into non-production environments, only adding or modifying as many files as required as opposed to a full deployment of the platform or any module. This team found it difficult to understand how virtual machines could be torn down and recreated.

Incidentally, this build and release team was responsible only for the non-production environments. The production environments were completely outsourced and managed by Singular, an infrastructure vendor. They had strict procedures for production releases. Chef was not one of their approved tools. In production set-ups, they used the conventional way of deployments using uDeploy. Operationally, this created challenges for all teams in that, until production, the teams used one form of deployment and an entirely different form for production. The challenge was further magnified because teams had been working in silos up until the last moment. Singular had no idea that Centos planned to use Chef for deployments until Centos had stabilized all of their release challenges in the non-production environments. The people at Singular needed to make transitions in their own minds on the new approach of automating Virtual Machines and making platform deployments before upgrading their skills and changing processes for production releases.

If Centos and Singular had worked as cross-functional teams, the move to automated environments would have been smoother.

On the bright side, this project gave us an opportunity to go back and look at our hardware. We realized a lot of machines weren't being used optimally. In Bangalore, we could reduce our hardware size by more than 50 percent just by asking hard questions and taking action based on the answers. This was done with absolutely no disruption to the activities underway. Of course, because a ramp-down was also in play, the amount of hardware necessary to support the ongoing platform was also less. The important point to remember is to dive deep into the hardware issue and find out what is absolutely necessary and what can go.

Things to Know and Do

- Infrastructure is a key element in ownership transfer, especially in situations involving transfer over geographies.

- Many organizations are transitioning to the cloud. An ownership transfer exercise during these times may create additional complexities. This brings additional focus to the infrastructure element of ownership transfer.

- Infrastructure-related costs and efforts are often underestimated in ownership transfer exercises. These can often double the cost of such exercises.

- It's important to engage the infrastructure teams early on during an ownership transfer exercise.

Chapter 9

Continuous Business

Why would one embark on an Ownership Transfer exercise? Because there is a need to change the status quo. There is a problem at some level, which needs addressing. It could be for any of the below reasons:

- The current team is not performing as desired.
- The costs of the program are too high.
- Geopolitical reasons make staying in the current location untenable.
- You need to reduce risk of being too dependent on a partner.
- It's the final phase of a build-operate-transfer (BOT).

Whatever the reason may be, the purpose of change is to improve and stabilize how the application supports business needs. However, the transfer process should not compromise the purpose for which it was created. Business needs must be met even when the transfer is in progress. This is what I mean by "continuous business."

The Float

Many of us have learned how to swim. We probably didn't attend swimming theory classes and then jump into the deep end of the pool. There was someone to guide us into the water. Slowly we got acclimatized to the water and its buoyancy. When we started with our first splashes, we had support. Someone or something ensured that we would float. That float was removed only after we gained capability and confidence.

Even so, we still don the float when we enter the deep end of the pool or choose to swim in unknown waters.

However, industry seems to think differently when it comes to functional projects. We somehow believe that a new team is capable of running a functional project with no assistance. The conventional thought is that both functional projects and ownership transfers cannot happen together. It is risky to try a functional project when a knowledge transfer is in play. Functional project execution is like treading into unknown waters for IT teams attempting it for the first time. You don't know where the currents are strong and where there could be hidden whirlpools. So, ask this question: Is it riskier to try a new functional project with a completely new set of owners, or is it riskier to try a functional project when the old guard is still around? The experienced members have greater knowledge and context and can provide the best opportunity to deliver a business critical project. We need the float. But then it is inconvenient. We would rather make the transition a success and then focus on business. In doing so, we end up making the project (ownership transfer) a success and the product (in this case, functional enhancement) a failure.

Transferring ownership takes a long time. Regular business cannot be paused for this activity. This means that you need to search deep to find that happy medium that will allow business to continue to function smoothly while a new pilot takes over. It's common for pilots to undergo on-the-job training flying commercial aircraft. Chances are, passengers would not know if the pilot is an ace or inexperienced. Many surgeries involve junior doctors assisting senior ones. Certainly, many of our applications are not that complex. We do not necessarily transfer ownership to someone who is less experienced or less skilled. That being said, any ownership transfer must involve a period of time when normal business operations continue with the old *and* new guard in play.

It's important to create the right perspective. At EuroT, we were not consumed by the fact that an ownership transfer exercise was going on. The entire organization was not crippled within this context. Instead, most parts of the organization continued to conduct their business normally. Projects flowed through the pipeline as they always would. We only interleaved those projects with the transfer exercise. So the organization as a whole saw things running as they normally would, but it was also aware of a large transfer program in progress. This is a new paradigm. We did not see the world through the lens of a transfer program. Our lens remained that of continuous business. The lens had just been tinted a little with the transfer program.

I look at continuous business from three different angles. The first one is about releases. A core tenet of Agile delivery is to make regular releases. A functionality built but not released provides no value. Instead, it gathers dust and runs the risk of requiring further changes. Hence, most organizations running on the Agile philosophy look to make regular releases. The next dimension of continuous business is delivering business value. Business-critical projects need to be executed. Management should not lose focus and fail to allocate resources to business critical projects. The core purpose of an IT organization is to conduct business. A transfer program must not get in the way of delivering business value. Perhaps the most important element of running a businesss is to ensure business continuity. Hence a transfer program should never be the reason for the application to crash in production.

Releases

Running an ownership transfer program is a bit like changing pilots when the plane is in flight. Projects continue to run, and the plane still flies, but the person running the project or piloting the aircraft changes mid-air. The important element here is that the plane should not crash. We can learn along the way, the plane can perhaps go a little slow, but at no point should it crash. For the initial phases of the EuroT project, the Bangalore team took responsibility for projects, but over time, the London teams took responsibility while continuing to have the Bangalore team for backup support. After having spent more than five years with the platform, the Bangalore team had become quite adept at ensuring business continuity.

The maximum risk of production issues centers around the timelines of releases. Release day and the two days following it are the riskiest days for a production fault to manifest. The release brings new pieces of code and configurations into the system. The chances are high that something will go wrong at the time of a release. System cache and memory have a tendency to build over time. An end-to-end perspective for an operation may involve transactions on the platform, followed by hand-offs to downstream systems for accounting and reconciliations. These hand-offs may take anywhere from a few hours to a few days to get fulfilled. You need to watch an entire lifecycle of a transaction to validate these.

At EuroT, we had a fairly rigorous process for making releases. Six weeks of development were followed by five weeks of performance and regression testing for the entire platform. During these periods, we tested the application end to end. We also validated for the downstream transactions. We had a separate environment for performance testing the application. These tests were used as a way to baseline the application performance and identify whether there might be potential issues coming up in the production systems. This entire set of activities taking place over a span of five weeks constituted a release.

Releases Are Must-Haves

Regular delivery is essential for an ownership transfer program to be a success. This is discussed in further detail in Chapter 12, "Measuring Ownership Transfer." We had five releases at EuroT as we went through the transfer program over ten months. In a sense, each release is like a pulse check on the program. The first release was expected to be uneventful because not a lot had been transferred over to London yet. Bangalore continued to own most of the components. As we moved to the second release, there were clear changes to the process. Some components had moved to London. The activity of release itself had to be modified to bring in members from both geographies.

By the time we moved on to the third release, the constitution of the team had changed rapidly. Each go-live was looked upon with bated breath. The end goal was to ensure we had a successful release. Our initial definition of success centered around the number and nature of faults we found, but we did not want to compromise on production releases. Faults could not occur on those. So, when go-lives occurred, there was particular focus on how they went. To our relief, all of our releases continued to run smoothly. Each passing release made everyone more confident that we were proceeding in the right direction. We could not have deemed this program a success without these releases.

Figure 9.1 gives a sense of how the team size changed over time. The entire transition went on for close to a year and, in that time, we had five releases. Each release was a checkpoint of the program health and team constitution.

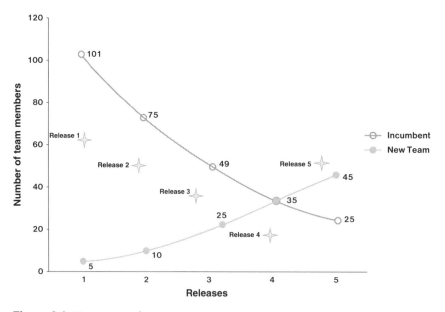

Figure 9.1 *Teams over releases*

The release processes were not necessarily simple. As we moved into the second and third releases, we observed that defects always came up during regression. To our pleasant surprise, the number of defects had not increased substantially. But we faced challenges related to how the defects would get addressed: specifically, who would address these defects. One thing we often dealt with was a defect that manifested as a result of a new feature. The London team would have developed a new feature, but the defect could have been a pre-existing issue in the code. The London team may have reused a defective component or their functionality may have surfaced the issue. The question became who would fix this defect. Some felt that because Bangalore had introduced this issue, they ought to fix it. Others believed that because London had taken ownership for this component, they ought to fix it. There is no one way to address such problems. Personalities drive a lot of what happens with such situations. In a few instances, the Bangalore team picked up the issue to fix it. Each time, the London team was made aware that specific Bangalore members would be rolling off of the project, so they would not be around for the next release. These tactical conversations drove home the point of what ownership actually entails.

Business Value

Functional projects are the best way to build knowledge. We actively looked for business-relevant projects to execute during this phase. In some cases, the IT team cajoled and pushed to get some projects executed just so we have something meaty to transfer ownership with. The business side was happy as well. Early on, they felt there was not adequate business value in executing some functional projects, but the need for the transformation program became the tipping point for project approval. This is a marked departure from the conventional relationships between business and IT. In most cases, IT teams find reasons (genuine, of course) why certain modules and features are complex and perhaps should not be attempted. During the EuroT ownership transfer, the IT team was actively encouraging the business teams to approve relevant projects for execution.

What Not to Transfer

As the IT teams and the business teams identified projects to transfer, we also realized several modules had had no new enhancements for years. One such module was the call center application. This module had not seen any enhancement for a while and there weren't many issues coming from this module. Most customers used the online reservation system and the online help to resolve most of their issues. The call center application had entered the autumn of its life. The IT group's discussion with business teams also validated this point. There were no further enhancements expected on this module. This prompted us to consider whether we should even spend time transferring over this particular application. This theme is explored further in Chapter 10, "Executing Ownership Transfer."

Business Stakeholder Management

New dimensions show up when we look at executing functional projects along with the transformation program. The team ownership changed at EuroT when we executed some projects. A team in Bangalore initially drove the project and, over time, the London team took over ownership. This required us to make adjustments to the communication processes. Although the Bangalore members started out conversing with the business teams, mid-stream, the points of contact changed from Bangalore to London. This can often create confusion for the business stakeholders. At EuroT, it helped that in most cases, the business analysts did not change through the entire course of the project. The same individual or individual pair (Bangalore and London) continued to work with the business teams. Development teams changed mid-way, but because a lot of the conversation with business was front-ended by the business analysts, continuity was maintained, even as the London business analysts picked up context and became more comfortable with the feature and with the business stakeholders.

Functionally heavy projects are a new business analyst's dream. Their job is not just to understand the functional domain. They also need to establish a healthy relationship with the business stakeholders because they will need to continuously interact with these folks to work through requirements and shepherd the features through user testing and acceptance. Delivering business value through the transition not only supports business purposes, but also enables the analysts to pick up context and become comfortable in executing their responsibilities.

In the latter phases, we had a couple of Bangalore team members travel to London. These provided a further sense of comfort for the business group. They perceived continuity and the only change was that the people with whom they were conversing earlier had traveled to London from Bangalore. At the same time, the London IT members were able to participate in these conversations with the business groups, thereby bringing down communication barriers for later projects. When provided with the right perspectives, the budgeting for this travel from Bangalore to London were also shared by the functional streams. In the case of sensitive exercises like ownership transfer, colocation adds disproportionate value.

Comfort through Continuous Business

In regular transfers, there is a great amount of stress placed on completing things within three months. A good part of it is because everything else tends to be put on hold while the knowledge transfer is taking place. This stress to complete the transfer quickly comes down several notches once the transfer teams are able to show that business value will not be compromised owing to the transfer. In effect the teams can plan the transfer over a longer duration. This extension of time helps the new team to proceed without taking undue risks. Releases occurring over time give additional confidence to the entire organization. More importantly, these functional projects are the only means for the business analysts of the new team to get their feet wet.

Teams need this float, especially during the most stressful periods of the year. For retail organizations, the most stressful time might be the November to December period. In the case of financial organizations, it would be the end of the financial year. These periods are peaks of activity around marketing, sales, and, in general, high traffic volumes on applications. This is much like coming across the rapids of a river. This is the period where the new team will value the float most. The ownership transfer program must ensure that this period is traversed as part of the transition. It provides new learning for the teams. It also provides reassurance to everyone that the new team can face further rapids.

Business Continuity

Most organizations have a very rigorous process for making releases. Even those organizations that are on the bleeding edge of continuous delivery have a sophisticated production release process. However, most of the activities have been automated, thereby bringing down the overheads on manual interventions. The EuroT release process was no different, but we had not yet reached a point of continuous delivery. The reason for release processes being heavyset is to ensure business continuity. This application, being the very soul of the organization, cannot afford to go down. It would be a breach of trust not just with contracted customers of EuroT, but also with the broad commuting population of Europe. The application simply must not go down. This tenet was deeply ingrained within every member of the company. Any program, however large it may be, is subservient to ensuring the production run of the application. Obviously, when we worked on the transfer program, we ensured this principle was strictly followed. This had a direct bearing on retaining and rolling off members within the program.

Production Support

Given production support is the most critical element, it is, perhaps, the last item that the new team should completely take over. This is not to say that the new team must not work on production issues in the interim, but it's a good idea to have the incumbent team available for tackling any production issues for a period of time. The responsibilities of the new team of a particular module could be broadly classified as

- Executing projects
- Making releases
- Interacting with stakeholders
- Supporting business activities
- Resolving issues in production

The new team can work on and build up confidence in picking up ownership for the first four responsibilities early on, but it is imperative for the incumbent to provide a safety net for at least two releases and assist in fixing any production issues until the team becomes confident and comfortable enough to handle production issues.

To that extent, this approach is similar to the Strangler approach on replacing legacy systems. In the system paradigm, the new system begins to handle the peripheral features and slowly moves in to take over the critical features in the center. It helps to discuss this from the incumbent's point of view. The incumbent relinquishes their presence for the first four responsibilities listed previously. Production support would be the last activity from which the incumbent would depart. But please note that I do not consider project execution and releases to be "peripheral" activities. They are very important in their own right. Production support, however, is in a different league. It is the oxygen that keeps the system running.

Team Ramp-Downs

While the ownership transfer process was moving ahead, we also had to plan for team ramp-downs in Bangalore. A large part of the transfer is about team members and their knowledge. More importantly, it is about the individual's motivations and interest. An ownership transfer exercise is not necessarily something that many people would be comfortable with. Typical knowledge workers prefer to work on projects where they can gain rather than give knowledge. From that standpoint, this exercise did not look that interesting to a lot of individuals. However, some members who had spent lots of time on the application were extremely important for this ownership transfer project. After all, these were the sources from which knowledge had to be transferred over. Besides, their tenure was essential to provide business continuity. Many conversations were needed with each member to discuss the opportunities and criticality of his or her continuity on the program.

While deciding on the ramp-down, we needed to look at which elements were being transferred. The broad plan was that the Bangalore side of the team that had knowledge of a certain area would be rolled off after that module had moved over. However, this was not a simple mapping exercise. We often had members who were adept at more than one area. We also wanted to ensure that senior members were part of the actual transfer exercise. Interacting with a different team from a different organization overseas will require maturity, especially given the nature of the exercise. Many of these aspects went into defining the ramp-down plan. We had to sit down with every member of the team to have these discussions. Ironically, after these discussions were done and the plan was put in place, it was time for the plan to change!

Some modules took longer than expected, or there was a change in the schedule of transfer. Some of the changes were driven by business projects that came our way. Team ramp-downs had to be continuously reexamined. We held weekly meetings to revisit team plans. Some London teams were concerned about losing a particular Bangalore team member even though the plan had been set and communicated in advance. These tactical situations required us to revisit our plans and have further conversations with individual team members. These are not easy discussions. It is difficult to keep changing a person's roll-off date time and again. Being Agile is not a reason to create uncertainty for individuals.

Ownership Transfer Must End as a Non-Event

How often have you seen transitions where on the last day of the activity, there are still a number of unfinished items? The old guard agrees to document and pass over the details to the new guard, who is still waiting for the last of the knowledge to be transferred. The last day of the exercise ends with a series of action items from both parties. This only means that the terms of the contract had ended, but not the transfer exercise itself. In our transactional world, we force-fit the contract clause to assume that the exercise is over. Troubles often begin soon thereafter. A release may not go successfully or defects occur in production. Frantic calls are made. Initial responses involve fault-finding and blame-placing. If the project is lucky, some members of the old guard come back for a period of time. In essence, the transfer exercise must be resumed.

When Business Continuity Is Compromised

Restins is a large player in the food services industry. They provide a broad range of fresh produce to large wholesalers, supermarkets, and restaurants. The advent of ecommerce has meant moving a large part of their daily operations online. Their clients can place orders, edit scheduled deliveries, and pay online. Of late, Restins's clients could also track the status of an order and how soon they can expect an order to reach its destination.

In 2012, Restins decided to outsource their IT operations to InfoIndia, a large India-based IT house. Per the advice and the strong assurance given by the sales teams of InfoIndia, Restins planned for a three-month transition period.

At the end of three months, InfoIndia took charge of the entire operation and Restins let go of most of their existing IT team members. In the fourth month, the InfoIndia team made a release into production. After the release, the Restins's website slowed down. Restins's clients began calling because they could not track their shipment. The call center employees could not respond to their clients either because their own version of the website had also become slow.

After a number of complaints, Restins' clients began ordering from other places. A lot of the trust and relationships Restins had created over time began to unravel in a single day. The account managers at Restins were sitting at their client's offices and providing assurances that everything would be back to normal within a day. However, the account managers had no idea how long it would actually take. In the fresh produce business, deliveries need to occur every day. Restins's clients wanted to know whether they could expect delivery the next day. Their issue was not the application. Their issue was in the consistent delivery of their product.

Back in the IT department, the Restins CIO, Jack Harper, had returned after a dressing-down from the CEO. The InfoIndia account manager, Aravind Panicker, smiled at him and said, "Sir, this is a minor blip. We will get it resolved by tomorrow. The problem is that the code base is not modularized."

Jack responded, "Aravind, that unmodularized code base just cost us two million dollars. You own that code base now. Please write us a check for two million."

Aravind began to wipe the beads of sweat rapidly forming on his brow. Jack Harper sighed and picked up his phone. He had to call each one of the Restins engineers he had let go.

An actual transfer exercise must end as a non-event. The transition over a period of time must occur in such a way that a closure becomes more of a formality than a contract-imposed timeline. At EuroT, we were lucky in this regard. After the initial four months of tumult, the program kicked into a mode where the transfer exercise had become *routine*. So it came as a surprise to many when we called for cake-cutting after 11 months. The program had seeped into people's minds so much that everyone viewed it as routine.

Things to Know and Do

- The new team needs the float when embarking on functional projects the first time.
- Releases are a key measure to ensure transfer occurs smoothly.
- Ensure the teams go through the peak seasons during the transition. This provides the most valuable learning for the teams.
- Teams must actively search for functional projects to aid in the transfer process.
- The more regular business is conducted normally, the less the stress on the ownership transfer program.
- Production support is the last activity from which the incumbent should step off. The incumbent safety net for production support must exist at least for two releases of that module/product.
- Team ramp-downs must take into account business continuity needs of the product.
- Ownership transfer may start as a major activity, but must end as a non-event.

Chapter 10

Executing Ownership Transfer

Ownership transfer does not debunk knowledge. After all, one cannot take ownership without appropriate knowledge. At EuroT, we spent quite a bit of time and effort in defining how knowledge and ownership would be transferred. In Bangalore, we came together and had sessions about how to involve the London teams on the ownership transfer. Bangalore looked at the London team as its customer. This made sense in that, by the end of the exercise, London should be satisfied and confident enough to take ownership.

Many discussions occurred about the methodology that would be followed. The original idea was to start with an inception phase. This phase establishes the broad contours of the project, contours such as its purpose, timelines, costs, and stakeholders. However, we had so many tracks to take on. It would be difficult to start off with a large-scale inception for this sort of an exercise. How would we know things were on track? How do you measure the efficacy of the transfer? Do we know what "good" looks like? A similar set of conversations occurred in London as well.

A quick point of congruence was on what *not* to transfer. All stakeholders were clear that just passing knowledge that was not actionable was a waste. People would forget what they had learnt if they didn't get to use that knowledge. I dread the time when I may have to help my son with his homework. I do not remember much of what we were taught in school. If we do not actively use our knowledge, we will lose it. We discovered there were areas of code owned by the Bangalore team that had not been modified for more than two years. In fact, no one in Bangalore had enough context or knowledge of it! If these pieces needed to be modified, even the old guard would need to learn something about the system before making changes. And, if Bangalore could learn and make changes on that piece of functionality, so could London. We made the decision not to spend our effort transferring these areas.

The Process of Transfer

In Chapter 4, we discussed breaking up the program into knowledge units (KU). We also established that code forms the central basis for knowledge transfer. The next point to consider is the process of transfer. At a broader level, the London and Bangalore teams had agreed to utilize existing projects as vehicles for knowledge transfer. We conducted a couple of exercises in London, predominantly to identify which teams ought to take ownership for which modules. When these had been defined, it paved the way for us to begin the transfer in earnest. The intent was to have the Bangalore team lead the feature for one release. At EuroT, one release comprised three iterations. Subsequent functionalities of the feature would be led by the London teams (see Figure 10.1). In the first phase, two members from London would work as part of the Bangalore team, and in the second phase, two members from Bangalore would work as part of the London team. The Bangalore team's involvement in the second phase ensured there was some help available in case of problems. In general, this bolstered the team's confidence.

We continued with the projects as normal except that when we moved into the IPMs (iteration planning meetings),[1] we decided to put extra focus on the transfer theme. There would be a story around ownership transfer as well. The intent was to look at every functional story and articulate the knowledge that could be gleaned by going over the story. At a fundamental level, we realized that it was possible to state

Ownership Transfer

Figure 10.1 *Project transition during ownership transfer*

---

1. www.agilesherpa.org/agile_coach/iteration/planning_meeting/

what needed to be taught, but difficult to state what would be learnt. What is learnt, of course, is more important than what is taught. However, we felt it was important to talk about the Ownership Transfer, so that the theme remained in the team's conscious memory.

Pairing

An unstated element through all the previous chapters is the notion of pair programming.[2] Pair programming can be considered the heartbeat of this program. If organizations do not have a culture of pairing, ownership transfer as enunciated in this book will not work. In many organizations, pairing is still considered a luxury. In fact, aside from EuroT, in every other ownership transfer situation I was involved with, pairing was considered a negotiable concept for management. In those cases, we needed to convince people of the benefits of pair programming in general before making a case for pair programming for ownership transfer. Luckily, there are many good materials to read about the benefits of pairing.[3] In a nutshell, these benefits include the following:

- When rigorously implemented, pairing removes the need for a code-review phase.
- Pairing ensures there are fewer defects identified during the QA phase.
- Productivity increases as members do not get bored and slack off.
- Risks and issues are surfaced earlier. Pairs tend to be more confident about conveying potential problems to leadership.
- Dependencies on individuals are drastically reduced.

At EuroT, we did not have the luxury of all our members being located in the same place during the time of the ownership transfer. There are difficulties and opportunities in every situation. When we started off with remote pairing, the London team was quite happy to work on the Bangalore schedule. They started their morning at 5.30 AM and finished off by 12.30 PM. Given this schedule, they worked from home. It helped the folks in London because they did not have to endure the commute to the office as long as the transfer process was going on. On the Bangalore side, the team was very conscious that their counterparts were getting up so early to pair with

---

2. http://guide.agilealliance.org/guide/pairing.html
3. http://c2.com/cgi/wiki?PairProgrammingBenefits

them. This made the team extremely considerate of their time. The team ensured that they did not get into unimportant meetings and synchronized their lunch times with London's breakfast.

Tracking Ownership Transfer

A lot of time was spent discussing criteria for measuring the efficacy of the process. The ownership transfer story we put within each iteration helped out. There were several reasons on how this ownership transfer story helped. On one hand, it helped us factor in the loss of velocity due to the transfer. It also allowed us to account for the effort and cost toward the transfer exercise. Identifying the criteria also allowed us to track what could realistically be accomplished within the transfer process.

However, we found defining the acceptance criteria for these stories difficult. There were also interesting tactical challenges around what would be showcased for the story and who would close out the story. After discussions with the London developers who had directly paired with developers in Bangalore, our approach eventually focused on closing the stories based on a set of questions:

- Are you comfortable enhancing this functionality on your own?
- Can you fix a regression defect that might arise in this module?
- Can you fix a production defect that might arise in this module?

While the story at a team level enabled us to track ownership transfer on the ground, chapter 12 on Measuring Ownership Transfer explores how ownership transfer can be assessed at a program level.

Teaming

In 1965, Bruce Tuckman, professor of educational psychology at The Ohio State University, proposed the stages of group development.[4] He proposed that teams needed to go through four phases: forming, storming, norming, and performing. The transfer exercise also deals with these multiple dimensions of complexity. In the case of EuroT, we had not been doing remote pairing prior to this ownership transfer exercise, but, on top of that, we would be working with faceless people from a

---

4. www.mindtools.com/pages/article/newLDR_86.htm

different country, geography, and organization. Even outside the structure of an ownership transfer, executing a regular project in these circumstances would have been challenging. Many of us do not appreciate the challenge of working in such an environment. We start the ownership exercise and begin interacting with a set of people that we are not yet comfortable with.

For a moment, let us ignore that a transfer exercise is in play and assume instead that it is a project requiring coordination between two teams with similar but not identical skill sets. Let us also assume that these teams are geographically dispersed and from different nationalities and organizations. The first thing to do is to evolve the team norms: Bring the teams together, make them gel, create an atmosphere of comfort and familiarity. When it comes to this type of an exercise, people have a tendency to rush through things. Rushing through this kind of exercise can be even more traumatic than regular projects. There will be strong undercurrents. But rather than acknowledge the elephant in the room, we act like it does not exist. A team forming-storming-norming exercise is critical. We need to discuss both the fears and concerns of the individuals in the team. These discussions can be cathartic and can lend themselves to stronger team bonds. Don't make the mistake of thinking that all knowledge can be transferred. There might always be that one disaster when you may need to call your old partner.

In the case of EuroT, we had a working relation of more than five years. Some of the Bangalore and London members had interacted on other projects prior to this, even though they had not met with each other in person. Even so, we still had a norming session for the first project via teleconference. The session helped break the ice and create an informal atmosphere. Although this meeting's benefits were not quantifiable, it helped a lot in terms of allowing people to reach out to each other. Apart from funny introductions, we also discussed stand-up timings, modalities around the stand-ups, pair timings, and so on. We also made sure that London and Bangalore developers spoke alternately. This ensured that members on both sides of the conversation were alert throughout the whole session.

Remote Pairing Checklist

Our stand-ups at EuroT were conducted on Google Hangouts. This was interesting and empowering. The novelty of using Hangouts made people interested enough to attend the stand-ups on time. Of course, we had the usual goof-ups of connections dropping or windows freezing, but being able to see the other person and perhaps even crack a joke with her went a long way toward creating an amiable environment. Several members found the experience valuable.

The first team found that they needed to try out different mechanisms and tools before making their choices. Based on this knowledge, we created a remote pairing checklist (Table 10-1) that could be used as a guide for other teams to follow. This was published on our intranet as well. Most teams began following many of these norms. We also began to make more conscious attempts to bring team members together in the same location.

Table 10-1 *Remote Pairing Checklist*

No	Item	Description
1	Team Norming	Start-off by having a session with all team members (from both sides) participating. Keep it fun and easy. It helps break barriers.
2	Retro	Conduct retros without fail to check what needs to change.
3	Working hours	London starts early and Bangalore starts late. Agree with the teams on working hours.
4	Stand-up time	Ensure stand-ups occur conveniently for people.
5	Team Viewer	Best tool for remote pairing.
6	Dedicated repo for the KT team (recommended because it aligned with program objective)	Where we are using a separate repo and pipeline (not impacting the core pipeline), this will help. This needs to be self-contained within the team.
7	KT story per iteration	Factor for loss in efficiency. We added a story for the purpose of KT. It accounts for knowledge getting transferred as part of the iteration. The acceptance criteria is read through by the appropriate members and closed when accepted.
8	Travel	Travel either from London or Bangalore. Bringing team members together is best!
9	Headsets	Obtain comfortable headsets. Headsets that cover the entire ear (circumaural) and noise-cancelling are the best.

The point about the headset is the result of taking feedback from the trenches. After the first retro, the team members were vehement about the need for good headsets. The leadership team was bemused by this and questioned the team. One of the engineers told us to sit for just two hours with our personal headset and chat with someone from London. No further questions were posed and the headsets were procured. Servant leadership does bring its own set of quirks.

When Organizational Policies Come in the Way

A year after the EuroT transfer, I was working with Triborg, a Fortune 50 organization. This organization was going through an internal ownership transfer as well. In this organization, stand-ups were done only via teleconferencing. Most freeware applications such as Skype and Google were not allowed within the organization network. When we suggested using some of these tools, middle management looked at us as if we were from another planet. We were only allowed to use corporate-approved tools. However, consultants could not access those tools and they did not receive laptops. Those were the policies and no one could question them. Incidentally. it was a profitable setup with a surplus budget for their IT division. Ownership transfer especially to an outsourced party is tenuous under these circumstances.

Retrospectives

The three-month templated knowledge transfer exercises do not lend themselves to retrospectives and course-correction. On the other hand, an ownership transfer exercise needs to run in the most Agile manner possible. By now, we would be well aware of the multitude of complexities and uncertainties facing such an exercise. Retrospectives play a large role in helping us learn and course-correct. Ownership transfer retrospectives are sensitive. There may be personnel from several different organizations or groups coming together to discuss what went right and what went wrong. These discussions can get ugly at one end of the scale or mute and ineffective on the other end. Running these retrospectives calls for maturity and significant facilitation skills. I strongly suggest that the most senior member of the IT organization, preferably the CIO, conducts the first few retrospectives. This will send a powerful message to the entire program.

In the case of EuroT, the development manager of a particular stream ran the retrospectives. The retrospectives themselves were conducted in a novel way because we were doing this in a distributed fashion. One retrospective was specifically about how remote pairing had been going and how the ownership transfer was faring with one of the teams. We wanted to determine the team's thoughts about issues, challenges, and what they felt should change. We used Google Hangouts again for the retrospective. As we proceeded, we realized that using a common document to capture points by everyone was more efficient. Everyone stopped speaking through the microphones and began typing out their points on the common document. Suddenly, the retrospective became silent. No one was speaking—instead everyone was updating the common document. Everyone put in their points on the shared document and voted with a "+1" for the points they supported.

The retrospective notes for one of the sessions is given here (names of people have been changed).

Overall Points

1. Initial loss in velocity as we were trying out a number of tools.

2. Time taken in the naming stuff, which we felt could have been spent better.

3. We have not thought about QA pairing. At the moment no QA is present to take the knowledge. This needs to be addressed.

4. Discussions on writing Integration Tests and team came up with good suggestions.

Lessons

1. Use the right tool for collaboration and start small.

2. People don't disturb you when remote pairing. So productivity seems to increase when you remote pair.

3. London developers can help in working with stakeholders in London.

4. Use the stand-up opportunity to do the dev huddle. Essentially continue normal Agile practices.

Who Said What

Astell, developer

- Screen sharing did not work so well earlier.

- Time difference is a bit of a problem. If it was a local team, we could have utilized time better.

- Look at our working hours once more—we are starting off early.

- Else things have worked well in terms of pairing.

- It made no difference. Fantastic bonding in any case.

- Teamviewer contributes to making this successful.

- Fully dedicated to the project.

- Naming stuff—bothered us a lot. Got stuck with the naming and it bothered us.

- People who raised the nomenclature issue raised it vigorously and then disappeared.

- Will have to start at 8 AM—cannot do 5 AM from next week.

Vinay, developer

- Earlier were experimenting with tools.

- Now that is stabilized.

- Pairing with Ravish and Astell was fruitful. Smooth in getting along with both of them.

- Astell and Ravish have started working early so we get more working time.

David, developer

- Naming of the repository took lots of time.

- Skype is working fine.

Ravish, developer

- Remote pairing—writing of tools etc. has been going well.

- Decision to generate deployers and maps in London—right now we are trying to deploy the code in Type 2 environment. This was a good decision.

- Choosing where to compile the code has given us a good boost.

- Pairing with Vinay and Sam is fun.

Sam, architect

- Not much more to add.

- Worked very smoothly.

- Skype and Teamviewer have been working well.

- Use of headphone for the whole day was getting tiring.

Although we ensured that these items were passed on to other teams for their transfer exercise, not all teams went through the same kind of experience. Another team involved in the transfer of a functional component faced more difficulties.

Given below is its retro notes. The names of both team members and components have been changed for privacy reasons.

We started off with a happiness radar[5] *to narrow down on the major area of concern. We started off with the categories People, Technology, and Process. The process of knowledge transfer that we're employing turned out to be the biggest reason for unhappiness. The people we're interacting with and the tools used in the process were of less concern.*

The team focused on the process for the rest of the retro. They categorized their thoughts based on whether they think we should drop, add, keep, or improve the various aspects of the process.

Drop:

- Making dev pairs part of the London team—For a couple of iterations, we had a dev pair from the London team pair with us. We drove a few stories in that time. Then a pair from here began to be considered a part of the London team. The dev pair here does not feel part of the team, and is not involved in most of the team's activities. The concerns that came out of this are:

- Standups not working—The dev pair from Bangalore have no context of what London is working on, besides the Journey[6] project. Most of the discussions in the standup are of no use to the Bangalore pair.

- No participation in IPMs—In the beginning, the Bangalore devs had no context of what stories were going to be played, because they were not involved in London's IPMs. Clarity was sought by asking for the link to the story wall.

- Sign-ups are not driven by London—Devs in London tend to pick up whichever stories they like. No priorities or dependencies are called out. No one informs the Bangalore pair about what stories are available for sign-up.

- Make own conclusions to develop—Scenarios covered in the stories are not exhaustive. The devs have to draw their own conclusions—even if they are sometimes contradictory to the story narrative—and develop based on these assumptions.

- Ad-hoc involvement of Bangalore QA—The QA from OM[7] is being pulled into Journey story testing in an ad-hoc manner. She is not given the context of the feature or story beforehand and is expected to pick up on the fly whenever questions come up.

Add:

- Define the scope of KT (dev+QA)—The scope of functional context that Bangalore is expected to impart is unclear. Should devs run through other flows that are not covered in the feature? The same holds for QAs. It started off as a context transfer of the automation framework. Slowly, the London QA started asking for help with Journey and a large part of the pairing time was spent on this.

---

5. www.funretrospectives.com/happiness-radar/
6. Name of a specific project in play at that time
7. Name of a specific team

- More facetime—The lack of trust and understanding between the pairs working remotely could be improved by having one party travel and work in person. Increased facetime will mean increased exposure and more points of contact to converse with. Video chats may be a good start to establish some familiarity.

- Let London pick up regression defects—The best way to explore code is to fix regression defects. Have the London team (pairing with the Bangalore devs at first) pick up defects.

- Expectation that KT time is meant for KT only—Sometimes, during pairing hours, the devs or QAs get pulled into meetings or work on other items. Focus on the KT item is lost. Waste of overlapping pairing time. E.g. a London dev new to pairing asked for time to set up the dev machine, instead of using already set-up pairing machines. Ate into a day's KT time.

- Scope of documentation—London devs asked for manuals and documents to help them understand the tools (e.g. SoapUI) and system. Is this under the scope of KT? Can they explore the resources that are already available and use those?

- Clarity on who is pairing from London—The rotation of London devs pairing with Bangalore devs is not clear. New devs have been joining, working for a day and changing pairs.

Keep:

- Using feature development to transfer context—As opposed to classroom sessions and/or extensive documentation.

- Giving context of build and deployment—The London devs are happy that alongside Web-Services context, they were also able to learn about the build and deployment processes, and would like to continue to do so.

- Dev setting context for London QA—The London dev gave the London QA context during the dev box. Early feedback could be captured this way.

Improve:

- Confidence on testing.

- Critical path testing for sign-off—The London QA finds out the critical path of the story and tests only that for sign-off. The edge cases are assumed to be tested during feature testing.

- Bangalore dev not involved in dev box testing—Dev box testing is carried out on the testing environment. The London dev drives it with the London QA. Bangalore is not involved.

- Tracking of KT—The KT cards being used to track progress are insufficient. Goals should be set at the start of the iteration, and clear acceptance criteria are to be added which can be signed off.

- Team involvement in planning of KT—The devs and QAs are not being involved in the actual planning and scoping of KT. Quicker feedback and different perspectives should be sought.

Note from retro facilitator: Getting feedback from London was not easy. So far, only one person has responded. More perspectives would have been nice. Quicker, regular feedback from them would be much more useful.

In the second retrospective, it was quite clear that the teams had not normed. The lack of trust is also evident in that all of the points are anonymously shared. Please note that in the first retrospective, the team was completely open about sharing their views and doing so under their own names. Although the second team had spoken a lot about the process and the challenges therein, the real issue was lack of trust. The underlying theme was that the team members had not gelled. This clearly showed in the way the retrospective itself panned out. Participation from the London teams was minimal. On the other hand, when the London team drove a retrospective, they did not get any participation from Bangalore.

It is always critical to identify the root cause of issues. In this case, we had team members with different worldviews and different expectations about this exercise. The team members were culturally divergent, and, in effect, we did not have a real team working on the transfer exercise. No amount of process and methodologies can make up for team misalignment. This further emphasizes the importance of team norming.

Ownership Transfer of BAs and QAs

At EuroT, with the first transfer already underway, we realized that we had not thought about the BAs and QAs at all. It was all fine to discuss transferring over the code, but you cannot realistically expect the QA back in Bangalore to continue testing what was being created in London. We needed to start remote pairing with QAs as well. Obvious as it may seem in hindsight, this did not initially occur to us during our first transfer. We were focused on putting a plan in place, getting the right tools, identifying what should be the first component to be transferred, and a number of other things. In this confusion, we missed out on the core enablers to software development—that is, requirements and quality assurance.

We had to quickly reassemble and ensure pairing between the BAs and QAs. When we started doing so, a number of interesting problems arose. In our specific instance, we had decided to break the components into services and user-interface layers. Some services were being transferred over as discrete products. Not all BAs and QAs had the technical skill to write service-specific stories and test services by themselves. There were a number of discussions about adding technical skills—improving the skills of the BAs and QAs in order to meet these requirements. Based on those discussions, specific training programs were created for BAs and the QAs. This also fed back into the hiring program of EuroT. By the end of the program, EuroT had hired five additional QA members with automation skills but had not added any new BAs to the team.

This is not an isolated instance. Management tends to look at BAs and QAs as an afterthought. In the ownership transfer exercise with Triborg, I advised management to think about ownership transfer for the QAs. Their refrain was "let us first address the developer issue. That normally comes first, doesn't it?" The problem with this approach is that you spend all your time addressing the development part of the transfer. The QA angle shows up well into the execution, often after the project's execution is half-complete. QA automation skills are the most underrated element in Agile projects. These problems continue to haunt ownership transfer programs as well.

Transferring Hardware

In most cases, ownership transfer also involves changes to capacity—either downsizing or, in some cases, upsizing. These changes to capacity will inevitably bring about structural changes. More of this is discussed in Chapter 11, "Process." Changes to team capacity also require concurrent changes to hardware capacity. Transferring hardware is an equally important tenet of ownership transfer. This played out quite strongly in the EuroT project.

We started with one team to transfer the build and deployment over to London. This team met with a number of issues. As we progressed with the build and deployment, we also worked around the creation of additional virtual machines in London. Ideally, the IS teams should have been the ones creating the virtual environment. However, given the development teams' orientation toward virtual machine automation, this was the team that started on the job. There was a lot of excitement because this was a novel experience for many developers.

However, we completely missed bringing the IS team—the team who owned the actual hardware—into the picture. Here was a set of development folks who started creating new virtual machines as part of the transfer exercise, but they never even interacted with the IS teams! As development teams, we focused more on how the machines would be created, what would be on those machines, and how to build the software for the machines. We did not think to ask whether there was adequate bandwidth within the IS teams to support those machines. Unfortunately, things that development teams do not normally deal with, such as anti-virus policy setups, were forgotten. It was only when we started looking for software licenses for a couple of our newly created virtual machines that we realized the challenges ahead.

Needless to say, this stream got stuck in the middle. The development and IS teams had to get together and align themselves with the ownership program. There was a period of stress and turmoil. The CIO had to intervene and include the IS team in the ownership transfer program. The IS teams raised many pertinent questions about supporting the hardware, determining which skills were required to maintain the automation, and of course, what to do with the existing non-virtualized hardware. The exercise became longer and much more complicated than previously envisaged. Having said that, two years after the transfer program, EuroT is firmly perched on the cloud, even for their production systems. Many of their modules make weekly releases. The virtual machine automation initiated by the developers and the build-and-deployment teams during the ownership transfer have proven to be valuable in the long term.

In hindsight, this transfer could have been planned better. The IS team, the build-and-deployment team, and the functional teams from London were critical stakeholders to this exercise. We had not accounted for all three constituents. This experience enforced the need to involve members within the first ring of orbit. Many organizations have separate teams handling infrastructure and the build-and-deployment teams. The knowledge and ownership of these groups also need to be transferred as part of the exercise. At the very minimum, the new team needs to have an appreciation of the hardware, build, and release processes.

Colocation

The original plan and budget for our program at EuroT did not account for colocation. Ironically, we had planned for the director and program manager to travel. But it became evident that many of our daily challenges required in-person interactions among team members. There was consistent demand for colocation emanating from the teams. Although such a choice may sound obvious, it still takes courage and agility for a program team to make the decision to have team members travel in such circumstances. The costs had not been accounted for earlier. But remember that the ownership transfer used commercial projects as vehicles for the transfer. The leaders of these commercial projects realized the value of colocation. The ownership program team and commercial project managers agreed about the need for colocation. Decisions were made for staff from Bangalore to travel to London and vice versa.

As we moved the program forward, a lot more people travelled from Bangalore to London. As the Bangalore members paired with London developers, the discussions became more London-centric due to the sheer fact that the development and transfer was occurring at London. Processes and practices aligned to suit London's manner of development and maintenance. At some level, this made more sense. The Bangalore members who became part of the London teams took on the role of subject matter experts.

What happened at EuroT is a pleasant deviation from what usually occurs during take-overs. In today's world, the new team goes to the incumbent's location and learns about the platform, but after they return to their home office, they face challenges such as lack of access rights and poor connectivity. These are obvious problems and can be easily handled. However, many challenges—such as working protocols and unwritten rules (driven by organizational culture)—can be subtle. The new team may find it difficult to get approvals because they might not know who to reach out to for approval and how to convince them. Decision-making often gets delayed and compromised. The client and the incumbent members must make it a point to work from the new team's premises for a period of time. This provides them with insights into the challenges faced by the new team. They will begin to appreciate real-time issues concerning network bandwidth, lack of access, and the cultural obstacles distance brings. That is how true customer collaboration works. Extending that a step further, the customer must try to bring over members from their business group to the new team's premises as well.

Changing Equations

Much of the ownership transfer process occurs in the mind. The team running the transfer program must appreciate this shift in the balance of power. Ownership demands empowerment. As the new team takes more ownership, they become more empowered as well. Simultaneously, the incumbent loses some of their empowerment. This can be a trying period, especially in cases where the same members have worked on the application together for years.

As we moved ahead with the EuroT transfer process, we faced a rather intriguing situation. The balance of ownership began to shift from Bangalore to London. This in itself, was expected and quite obvious; in fact, we had planned for this type of transition. With the first project, we created a process by which the Bangalore team owned the feature for the first release, and the London team picked up ownership from the second release. After a couple of months, London had already picked up ownership for a few areas. So we had a situation where, in some areas, Bangalore would completely own the piece, whereas in other areas, Bangalore was doing an active transfer with London, and still other areas in which London completely owned the piece. We had the good sense to plan this upfront and laid out our expectations quite clearly. This ensured that the project went smoothly, albeit with a higher level of overhead.

With the next commercial project, London had significantly picked up lots of areas on the transfer canvas, but there were some genuine concerns about their level of confidence. Although London had taken ownership for their areas of code, we added a general rule that anyone could make changes to the code. The caveat was that the person making the changes needed to let the owners of the code know about the changes, either before, during, or after making them. We intentionally left this open-ended so that individuals could make what they felt to be appropriate decisions on seeking counsel before changing the code. This was specifically done with the Bangalore developers in mind. For five years, the team in Bangalore had owned these areas of the application. The newly added rule of needing to seek permission from another person to change that code was a smack to their egos. For this reason, we made the decision to have developers decide for themselves about the code changes. If something was a small enough change, with few ramifications, the Bangalore folks could make the changes then inform London. If a change was significant and impacted several areas, it became necessary to inform, and perhaps also pair, with the London folks.

We had several difficult conversations during the course of this project. Much of this was because the Bangalore team had a hard time reconciling their change of status. The developers were loath to inform London or consult with them about changes being made. Several changes had been made by the Bangalore developers without informing London, but their reticence to communicate had a bigger fallout. After a week, the developers in Bangalore realized that the repository into which they were checking-in was no longer being used by the London team. London had created their own repository for this piece of the code and was using that for their check-ins. Because there was no communication between the teams, the London folks, being the owners, decided to move the repository to improve their efficiency. It came as a rude shock to both sides. We had some testy discussions about process, responsibility, ownership, and just finding faults. The crux of the matter was really a lack of communication. Thankfully, the amount of rework was manageable.

The next project had far more stringent guidelines on who could make changes to the code. Some of the London teams preferred for Bangalore not to make any changes to the code. Other London teams were more open to keeping Bangalore involved. The frustration on the teams in Bangalore increased. Many folks felt that there were easier ways to write the code, or noticed what, according to them, were obvious mistakes. But they did not have the freedom to change things on their own. As difficult it is to take up ownership, it is equally difficult to give up ownership. Bangalore needed to realize that things had moved on, and there was someone else beside them who should be losing sleep over what happened to the application.

By the time we reached the nine-month mark, only London was making changes to the code. The repository was locked so other members of the team could not check-in any code. This was what had been planned for the eventual status. At this point, ownership had well and truly transferred over. London had built unique context with the platform. There were things now that London knew that Bangalore did not. This change in situation made it far easier for teams to accept the new scheme of things.

But the ramifications on the ground were not that apparent until we actually experienced them. From the perspective of Bangalore, the members were initially excited. The developers looked upon themselves as teachers who had to impart knowledge to students. Over time, these developers had to step down from their pedestals and work with the London developers on an equal footing. Over time, the Bangalore developer's role dwindled further to just being called only when there was a need or, in some instances, only as a backup. Eventually, these developers weren't needed at all.

In the case of the London members, the opposite effect was felt. For the first project, they looked upon themselves as customers. With that in mind, they started with a slightly hands-off approach. Over time, they became reluctant students. They had to pick up more responsibility and understand the innards of the application. As time went on, they needed to understand not only what was happening at the moment, but also everything that had happened since the time the application was created. In time, they took responsibility for all the technical debt existing in the code apart from the regression defects. Eventually London picked up ownership for the entire application and the students became the teachers.

Figure 10.2 provides a view on how the sense of ownership evolves amongst both the incumbent team and the team that is taking over. As teams progress with the transition, a parallel mind shift occurs amongst members as well.

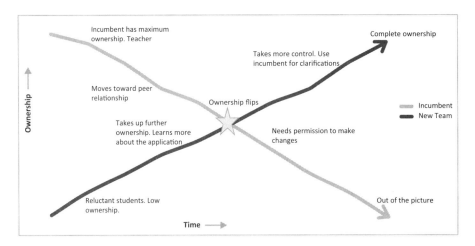

Figure 10.2 *Mindshift–ownership over time*

A Layered Experience

Projects and experiences play out at multiple levels. At the lowest level are two team members interacting. At the highest level are two organizations determining the direction of the transfer. In between lie a myriad of layers that provide perspectives at various levels of abstractions. Our transfer exercise at EuroT was deemed successful. The transfer occurred within budget and on time. Most of the original objectives were fulfilled. The EuroT CEO made it a point to thank ThoughtWorks at multiple levels for helping lead the program toward its eventual success.

Different members had varying experiences. Some members found the experience exhilarating. One of the BAs from Bangalore mentioned that playing the BA role for Bangalore and London and facilitating discussions across geographies was an extremely rich and valuable experience. This was despite the fact that she had to work very long hours for a period of time. Similarly, one of the developers from London mentioned that remote pairing had been the best experience in his fairly long professional career. Getting to interact with some of the senior members of the Bangalore team had been a valuable experience.

There were also those who found the experience tiring and tenuous. Several members found it difficult to work remotely. People's opinions and working styles had not always matched. For some, the transfer itself did not make sense. Many did not like the new arrangement. Even four months after the transfer was completed, some felt that things were not completely settled. But with each passing day, the foundations of the new dispensation settles in that much more. Time will eventually cement the contours of the new structure.

Things to Know and Do

- Pairing is a key concept for ownership transfer.

- What is being learnt is more important than what is being taught.

- Use existing projects as vehicles of ownership transfer.

- Team norming is critical before starting the ownership transfer.

- Business analysts' (BA) and quality analysts' (QA) ownership transfer are as important as that of developers. These cannot be delayed.

- Hardware transfer needs to be executed in parallel with the software transfer.

- The infrastructure, build, and deploy teams need to be involved in the exercise right from the beginning.

- The incumbent must treat the new team as their customer. The new team should be satisfied and confident enough to take ownership by the end of the exercise.

- Giving away is equally difficult. Ensure the incumbent member's sentiments are honored.

- Nothing works like colocation. Be open to colocation travel.

- The client and the incumbent must occasionally work from the new team's location to appreciate constraints better.

Intra Company Transfer—A Success Story

ThoughtWorks had been working with a gaming organization, Sports Lotteri for over three years. This company had been in business for nearly a hundred years. They realized the need to refresh their entire product offering for two major reasons: Their loyal set of customers was dying, which was understandable for a hundred-year-old company. Plus, their existing systems were tough to change, given the legacy tools driving their platform. When these systems were built thirty years earlier, they followed the latest technology of the time. However, time and the evolving nature of the market forced Sports Lotteri to change the engine that drove their platform.

(continued)

The ThoughtWorks team partnering this customer was based out of Pune, a thriving city in the western part of India. Over time, the needs of the customer started to grow, but the Pune setup did not have enough people to support the rapid growth of the Sports Lotteri project. At the same time, ThoughtWorks was setting up an office in Gurgaon, a suburb of New Delhi. Given this facility was just being set up, the office had the capacity to absorb and grow an account like the Sports Lotteri.

After some discussion with their customer, ThoughtWorks decided to move the project location to Gurgaon. Some of the staff from Gurgaon came down to the Pune office. The team started off by pairing with the existing team members. When they started pairing, the new team had difficulty understanding the domain. The Pune lead set up a number of KT sessions to help the Gurgaon team understand the business background and the functional logic of the platform. The pairing and KT sessions started in the month of November.

After about three months, the entire team moved over to Gurgaon. During these initial three months, the Infrastructure team worked through and ensured the right sets of VPN connectivity were established from Gurgaon to the client networks.

The entire set of Pune members initially went over to Gurgaon and additional members joined in the Gurgaon office. The full team at this point was almost double its original size. They worked together for a period of four months.

The ThoughtWorks team had a commitment to the customer to release a major product upgrade by the end of July. Their ownership transfer could not be a reason for this release to backfire. This team was set-up to make releases every week. However, due to operational constraints at the client end, the new features had to be toggled off when they went live. The team called these releases "black releases". The code was in production, but it was toggled off.

At the client's request, some of the features were turned on in April. After this, the team discovered a few issues, one of which was a major one related to system configuration. The team was able to toggle off that feature immediately. Within a week, the team fixed it and made another release.

(continued)

After going live in April, all of the Pune members save one returned from Gurgaon. This member stayed back to ensure a smooth final release. The final release went live on August 14th instead of the end of July. The team missed their deadline by two weeks. However, in the grand scheme of things, the entire project had run smoothly, even with the ownership transfer coming in between. The successful transfer involved pair programming among developers and close pairing among BAs and QAs. The Pune team member returned to his home office two weeks after the live date in August.

The Gurgaon team expanded their team over the ensuing months by about fifty percent. This transfer involved only members within the same organization, yet it took more than nine months to execute successfully.

Chapter 11

Process

A process is a way to get things done. If we do something the same way again and again, we call it a process. Many of us know what these processes are with respect to software development. We even have certifications that assess and validate organizations on the maturity of their software processes. However, this chapter does not look at processes from the perspective of certifications. Agile puts people and interactions above processes. When a new team takes over, then, processes inevitably will change. After all, following a process cannot by itself be a successful outcome. Creating the right product is the true measure of success.

Sometimes we don't even realize that we have set up a process. Someone starts doing things in a certain way. Others find that method useful and begin to adopt it. This group then tells another group how they operate and describes its benefits. Thus a process slowly forms. In most Agile teams, processes are defined by members within teams. What begins as a practice within a community becomes a rigorous routine before anyone realizes it. It then becomes the only way to get things done. A process is born.

Team Interdependencies

A large organization will have a number of teams with unique responsibilities. How these teams interact can become a process in itself. It can form when specific teams need to depend on their counterparts to deliver pieces that will allow them to deliver their own part. Consider the release process as an example. Many organizations have a release manager. However, the release manager cannot make a release in isolation. The development team who created the product plays a critical role in making the release. Although the release manager may run the activity of releasing the product, she needs to obtain the time, support, and expertise of other teams to make this a reality. This activity of getting time and bandwidth from the development teams calls for a process.

But when the development teams have changed hands, we will need to re-look at that process. The earlier ways of working may not make sense for the new team. At EuroT, we had a distributed team. This meant more organized meetings, reports, and walkthroughs prior to the release. With the responsibility shifting over to London, communication became far more seamless. We did not have to rely on reports and meetings as much to communicate as we used to. The London teams were involved in earlier conversations about the modules that traditionally rested with them. With the change of hands, we merely needed to extend these conversations that London developers already had with the release team. So in this case, the release process became much more simplified.

Team Structure Changes

When you have feature teams, the same team works on every piece of the code to realize that feature. In effect, a set of seven to twelve team members will take complete ownership for delivering that piece of the project. It wouldn't matter if they have worked in that area before. The biggest benefits of this structure are that

- Ownership is concentrated within a single team.

- Focus remains high for the most part, because this team does nothing else but work on this one project.

- Communication overhead decreases to a minimum because all interactions are limited to a set of people.

The disadvantages, however, with this approach are

- Knowledge of the system in that particular area is less comprehensive. The team may spend extra effort because it is not comfortable with the code base.

- There is a likely chance for regression defects. A rigorous and thorough automation suite is a critical safety net.

With feature teams, stories are created through a vertical splice. That means that the team creates a story without considering whether it requires a service change, a dB change, or a front-end change. If the development and testing pair need to make changes to any or all of the components, then so be it.

In the case of product teams, each team focuses on the work that comes just within their area of responsibility. With this approach, the teams

- Build unique and deep knowledge over time.
- Have a greater understanding of the impact to enhancements and changes.
- Have a higher level of confidence in their ability to execute.
- Expend less effort to execute their part.

However,

- There is no one team that takes ownership for the entire project. There could be as many as four different teams working on a single project.
- One may require the project/program management support team to pull all these pieces together. This can call for greater overheads
- Based on how the product teams are structured, stories may be split differently. You will need to create stories that are well encapsulated for each product team. What was once a single story cutting through all the layers of architecture may become three stories. This could mean more effort is needed from the team in order to execute the project.

For the new dispensation at EuroT, we decided to have specific teams look after specific modules. The idea was to create deep skills and familiarity as well as ownership. The platform had become very large. Most large e-commerce platforms such as Amazon, eBay, or Google, are structured around product lines. You cannot expect a developer or a tester to swim through any part of the ocean with the same level of dexterity. Some places are deeper, some places have crashing waves, and some are colder. You would need deep familiarity to navigate these waters. The teams in London were already comfortable with this model of working. Because they were picking up most of the ownership, it made sense to modify team structures to suit their needs. This changed the way we ran projects.

Each ownership transfer brings in changes unique unto itself. It is a function of the eco-system, culture, and the organizational setup of the constituents. However, I am certain that that through these examples, you will be able to appreciate the type of process changes you may be required to undertake.

Inceptions and Project Ownership

The first set of changes occurs around inceptions. In the earlier scheme of things, one team owned delivery of the whole project. With ownership being split, different teams needed to be part of the inception. However, each team was not working on a single project. With feature teams, the entire focus for that team revolved around that particular feature. With the move to product teams, the team may be working on more than one feature or product at a time. The team's focus within a project could weaken. It becomes a challenge for the project manager to get people from different teams to come in for an inception. With divided attention, not all of the discussions within an inception may appeal to every member of the team.

At EuroT, we decided to identify a preeminent team to own the feature. Even though this team may not have been able to make all the necessary code changes, it was still important to ensure that one team took the customer's pulse and passed the information on to the other development teams. In this case, it made natural sense for the channel team to take ownership. The term *channel team* refers to the area of the platform through which the service, product, or benefit reaches the end customer. For most customer-facing developments, this team ends up being the website, mobile, or call center team.

This team then acted as a customer to the downstream teams. The channel team captured the overall business purposes, breaking them down into appropriate stories for the different teams that make up the entire project. The requirements thus passed on would then be showcased back to members within the channel team.

Instance of Ownership Transfer Introducing Process Rigor

Bills and Hamilton Consulting (BHC) is a large consulting firm advising some of the largest corporates and powerful government sectors. They engaged with ThoughtWorks to transform the way they managed a number of their consulting-oriented software products. After ThoughtWorks took over the engagement, we realized that the client organization did not have a set order for releases. In fact, the BHC team had let the duration of a sprint to be fluid. One sprint could last two weeks and the next one could go for six weeks! This goes against the core tenet of Agile. If anything, an Agile set-up will always stick with a specific duration for a sprint. This definition of a sprint is always sacrosanct. Several articles tell us why we should have fixed-time duration.[a] Broadly, fixed-time durations allow

---

a. http://www.agilitysw.com/blog/31-scrum-whys-fixed-length-sprints

- A regular cadence to develop and demo

- Consistency to track value and velocity

- Maintenance of the team's agility

- Creation of a self-reinforcing productive rhythm for the team as well as for all stakeholders

After ThoughtWorks took over, we defined a sprint to be of a fixed duration. In the beginning, we agreed to have sprints of four-week durations. The BHC team had developed many features but never put them into production. We needed to bring in processes to ensure that at the end of each sprint what had been developed actually went into production.

With the introduction of the new team, processes changed in three different areas:

- Cadence for releases

- Fixed-length sprints

- Processes that ensure developed features go into production at the earliest possible time

We realized that along with this arrangement, we needed to have a core set of people to provide ownership for the feature from an end-to-end perspective. We identified both a feature BA and a technical lead who would liaise with all the teams. These two individuals, along with the project manager, became the core for delivering the project. The feature BA and the tech lead were not new members added to the team. Already-existing team members took on extra responsibilities to play this additional role. In many cases, these members were the BAs and the lead developer of the channel team.

Skill Sets

Part of the change in process may also revolve around skill sets. Skill sets are important not just for developers. In strongly Agile fluent teams,[1] members who play both business analyst roles and quality analyst roles need a level of technical

---

1. http://martinfowler.com/articles/agileFluency.html

expertise. (Agile fluency is discussed further in Chapter 13, "The Three Bridges.") In our particular example, for those teams that owned specific services, the stories and acceptance criteria became fairly technical. There were no browser pages for this team to validate their changes. This meant that the BAs needed to get comfortable looking at and validating XML responses as a way of meeting acceptance criteria. Similarly, QAs found that they needed to write service tests as opposed to functional automation tests. Such instances are bound to occur in varying degrees in ownership transfer exercises. In fact, constraints surrounding skill sets can impact the entire direction of the transfer program. Whether one divides the new product vertically, horizontally, or using a matrix format may depend on the skill sets of the new team. When the new team or organization realizes the gap in skill, there is an urge to acquire talent either from the incumbent or from the market. As mentioned earlier, EuroT hired 6 automation QA engineers during the 10-month phase of the transfer.

Showcases

At EuroT, we had set iterations for every two weeks. Our showcases would occur at any given point during those two weeks. When stories were ready to be demoed, the BA, QA, and developers would showcase them to the product owner. There were also mega showcases which occurred when larger parts of a feature were completed. The product owner would usually do this for the project sponsor and for members in the steering committee. However, with the transition, our showcases needed to change. The stakeholders changed for different teams. For the teams implementing services, the customers were not the business users, but another team who would use the services. In fact, while development and testing continued, there was a need to collaborate with other teams. This was not easy. Firstly, the tenor of showcases changed. Some showcases became fairly technical, especially for the teams running the services components. It was also a change in role for the members of the consuming team. The teams doing development and demos also had to don the hat of consumers/recipients. The feature tech lead and feature BA needed to play crucial roles in enabling these activities.

Project Execution

The execution phase of the program is bound to see a transition. As processes switch from the old guard to the new, the projects executed in the interim experience higher levels of overhead. When there is a change in geography and a need to shift infrastructure, some of these challenges are amplified. Development teams need to make sure that after the code is checked-in, the builds on both geographies are green (meaning the builds in both Bangalore and London do not break). Some of these aspects can cause lots of difficulty with a distributed model plus the additional task of being responsible for someone else's work.

The challenges in coordinating four different teams to push out one feature cannot be overstated. Each team has their own view of the way the overall design and architecture should look. There will be ideas and points-of-view on where the business logic should reside—whether it should reside on the front-end or in the services. If the logic needs to be applied to the services, this calls for additional communication overheads from a functional perspective. The BAs of the front-end team work with the business groups to understand the business logic. This logic needs to be transferred over to the BAs from the services team. In an ideal situation, both the BAs should work in tandem and plan for joint sessions with the business team. However, these points are easier said than done.

Another core element of execution is testing. Ownership transfer brings changes to testing processes depending upon the philosophy of the new entity. During the development phase, Agile teams put tremendous focus on automation. The definition of a completed story is almost always something that has been developed, tested, and is now ready to be put into production. However, there are several practical nuances within this larger philosophy. For starters, unit tests are typically created by developers as they write the functional code. Many mature Agile organizations use test-driven development (TDD), wherein the developers write the test cases before writing the actual code. Then there are service tests and functional tests that test slightly larger components of functionality. Most organizations follow a pyramid structure of testing with the unit tests at the bottom of the pyramid and progress upwards to service tests, component tests, and user-interface-level functional tests. Each gradation of testing provides a higher level of abstraction with respect to the confidence in the code. These tests also run differently in different environments. The unit tests, which run at the most granular level, are typically run during code compilation. Other tests can be run at any time from the moment of triggering the build to a manual run after deployment into a test environment. The decisions on when these tests are run depend a lot on the culture of the group as well as the risk appetite of the group. Often, it is a strong function of the skill sets within the group to create and maintain a large suite of automation tests.

Defects

Any fault in the code will eventually manifest on the front end. In a sense, the QAs of the front-end team are responsible for the entire feature. If an issue identified in the application manifested due to a service-related fault, this reflects poorly on the testing rigor of the services team. Conversations on these issues can become confrontational. At EuroT, we encountered several defects that did not fit into any team's scheme of things. With the move to a product-based approach, every team wanted to move defects out of their bucket. The channel team (the team which handles the website, call center, or the mobile channels) would be the recipient of the reports of most defects, mostly because that is where almost all defects eventually surface. People who identified these defects would log them against one of these channels. What happens under the hood is not relevant for black-box testers. So the channel team needed to spend time sifting through these defects, do an initial analysis, and assign it to the appropriate downstream teams. This became an additional routine for the channel team members. A triage team was created, made up of members from various teams. This team sifted through defects, identified their severity, and handed it off to the appropriate team. Before the transfer exercise, this type of process was not required.

Example of a Testing Process Change

We had an interesting conversation during the EuroT project about the point at which we should receive feedback on code. Within the current scheme, there was a set of smoke tests that were triggered the moment any code was checked-in. These consisted of about thirty-odd test cases that represented core scenarios in the application. Scenarios such as making, modifying, and cancelling a booking were typical test cases. The new team did not want these test cases run for every check-in. They felt it was more prudent to deploy the code on a test environment and run the smoke tests. They felt it was better to consolidate a bunch of check-ins and run the smoke tests at one go. This is a change in the development process, one that aligned with the comfort level of the new team. However, making this change during the process of transition, when we had members from the old team as well as the new team, was not an easy exercise. The older members needed to accept a change in a process that had been in vogue for a very long time.

Release Process

Every organization has a unique way of handling releases. Some groups make entire platform releases. In other organizations, releases are made for unique features or discrete technical components. Some organizations adopt the concept of release trains. This is a large area of study in itself and is a rapidly evolving area in the field of software development. The release train concept is largely process- and practice-driven. It forces teams to break features down into valuable blocks that can fit into a release timeline. It also enables teams to work within set timelines. Essentially, it molds team behavior by injecting discipline into release cadence.[2] However, the concept of continuous delivery changes the paradigm completely. It creates an ecosystem that allows organizations to release at will, but this ecosystem has a very strong engineering dimension.

When ownership for the platform is transferred, changes in the release process are to be expected. The new team may change the duration of the releases or the time and day of releases. The team may choose to move away from a platform release to discrete component releases. The new team may usher in the philosophy of continuous delivery as opposed to release trains. The parties involved in the releases will most certainly change. Getting the release teams to be part of the transfer plan is essential. From the first release, changes are bound to occur and getting this team's buy-in is crucial. At EuroT, before the ownership transfer, we had a release manager working out of Bangalore. As we continued through the transition, we needed to eliminate this role in our Bangalore location and transfer the responsibility to someone in London. This handover was executed through pairing over several releases.

Team Size Changes

No transfer exercise is complete without changes to the team size. Very seldom will we see an exercise where a hundred people are replaced with another hundred. More often than not, the team size reduces. Where an offshore element is introduced, the team size may actually increase. Communication overheads and cultural and language differences normally drive management to create additional interfacing layers. Team structures change when there is a change in team size. In a team of a hundred and fifty people, there could be a dedicated set of performance teams, automation teams, and build-and-deploy teams. When the number of team members is reduced, these can't be retained as independent teams. The responsibilities would need to be shared among a smaller set of individuals. These structural changes bring in other changes as well. While the team size has decreased, the application size remains the same. So teams with added responsibilities will need to get smarter in determining their roles. Further automations and smarter test runs become the order of the day. Teams would also need to look at all of their activities holistically and prune those that do not add as much value.

---

2. http://leadingagileteams.com/2015/02/09/5-benefits-of-the-agile-release-train-for-a-single-team/

As team sizes change, there will be a redefinition of responsibilities amongst teams. Before a release, large programs may require additional levels of validation for the entire platform. These may comprise of a series of regression runs in addition to any non-functional testing. Although most of these should be completed within the ambit of stories, this may not necessarily occur. Some of these activities rely heavily on infrastructure. Running performance tests and long sets of regression require dedicated and powerful test environments. Organizations invest in these items differently based upon the value propositions they perceive. When there is a reduction in the team capacity, you need to rethink who will run these activities. With 150 people, it was possible to have separate teams for performance testing and regression runs, but this cannot be the case when the team size is reduced by more than half. At the same time. you cannot do away with these runs entirely because they provide value to the platform. The team needs to keep in mind that the product itself is not decreasing in size.

In the case of EuroT, we absorbed these members within functional streams. We took another look at the entire gamut of performance scripts. The engineering side of the transformation had given us an opportunity to break down the monolith into discrete components. We used the same principle to break the performance scripts down as well. Teams picked up the responsibility of running discrete performance scripts based on the changes they were making to the code. The performance engineers picked up functional responsibilities when they were not running their testing. Automation scripts were handed over to the channel teams. The QAs took over responsibility for running, enhancing, and reporting on the automation scripts for the whole platform. It is to be noted that when there is a reduction in team size, appropriate mentoring will be needed for the assimilated team members so they are in a position to step-up and handle these additional responsibilities.

Conway's Law

Most organizations are real-world examples of Conway's Law. He states that "organizations which design systems ... are constrained to produce designs which are copies of the communication structures of these organizations."[3] Moving from a feature-centric team structure to a product-centric structure is an example of this process. Upon moving to a product-centric structure, we are bound to observe discrete layers in the design that will bear the signature of each product team.

---

3. https://en.wikipedia.org/wiki/Conway%27s_law

> ### Large Organization Software Release Process
>
> Large organizations tend to have deeply segmented groups. In a large Fortune 100 company, releasing a personalization module involves interacting with as many as fifteen different groups. Interestingly, this module may be visited by less than two percent of their customers. The organization structure does not give any leeway to redefine working modalities. We must follow the same path to production irrespective of the size and complexity of the software. The fifteen groups define the communication structure and thereby the process of the software release.

At EuroT, we had an internal team handling the non-production hardware and an external vendor taking responsibility for production hardware. The internal teams had limited access rights to deploy on the external systems. This meant that we had to interact closely with the external vendor for deployment. It took us nearly six weeks to stabilize the environment for external release.

The Definition of Done

Most Agile teams will grapple with this terminology at some point or the other.[4] In large enterprise programs, the senior leadership tries to bring in some level of consistency across teams through the notion of a standard *definition of done (DoD)*. Consequently, this is one term that also challenges the true empowerment of teams. So what is the "definition of done?" In short, it is a list of items that the team agrees must be completed to be able to announce that a story or a product is considered "done." These are not the same as the acceptance criteria for stories. The acceptance criteria are, most often, functional aspects. The "definition of done" checklist also contains items such as unit test coverage, regression, non-functional testing, documentation, and user training. All of these items are important when creating a potentially shippable product. Needless to say, when we switch over ownership, the DoD can change between teams. Often, the change is not so noticeable as to remove an item from the checklist. However, the level of rigor provided will likely change from team to team. Every team identifies and works with a set of DoD that makes the most sense to them. However, this cannot hamper the product integrity. That is another reason why we maintain that transfer ought to occur over a period of time. As teams discuss and debate what should constitute the DoD, the experience gained from making releases will also add to those insights.

---

4. https://www.scrumalliance.org/community/articles/2008/september/what-is-definition-of-done-(dod)

The Importance of the Definition of Done

Sati Inc., a large airline products company, was embarking on its journey of Agile transformation. Many of its employees had undergone three-day sessions on Scrum and Agile. This organization had also partnered with MyndLives, a strong offshore organization based out of India. The clients did a great job of defining and communicating the definition of done (DoD). The sprints commenced, but the team did not have a base-test environment. Sati Inc. instructed the MyndLives engineers to proceed and test on the developer boxes. Although everyone had agreed that the DoD required that the testing occur in the QA environment, Sati Inc. wanted to postpone that particular activity during the first sprint. There were some challenges with procuring and setting up the QA environment. One sprint followed another. Testers were doing all of their testing on the developer's boxes. This meant that developers and testers had to share their boxes. It's a bit like two people having to share a limited amount of food from the same plate. Ultimately, both remain hungry. Both the developers and testers felt rushed.

This created further anti-patterns. The unit test coverage was not at acceptable limits. The QAs regularly found issues. Things that worked one day were breaking the next day. Because it was technically a development environment, the developers made rapid changes to suit their purposes. The QAs had to repeat their tests again and again. Automation scripting was compromised because the QAs were spending most of their time in manual testing. By the end of four iterations, the teams had closed on none of their stories.

Sati Inc. became very annoyed with MyndLives. The matter was escalated. When MyndLives raised the point about environments, Sati Inc. refused to accept that all of the issues were because of lack of QA environment. MyndLives got into a retrospective with the senior leadership at Sati. The leadership team sat together and went over each line item on the definition of done. The team explained how each item on the list could be mapped back to the lack of the test environment.

This situation illustrates just how important it is for the IT leadership to track and facilitate the definition of done in large enterprise programs.

Production Support

How would the support process change with the advent of new teams? In a sense, it is intrinsically linked to releases. Releases are trigger points for production issues. New code, new configurations, and new functionalities appear during and in the immediate aftermath of a release. Nothing is more critical than addressing production issues on applications. Most knowledge transfer programs put a lot of focus in this area. However, within the context of an ownership transfer, production support ends up being just one piece of the larger puzzle. However, the philosophy of pairing is highest in production support. Debugging issues require a lot of experience and context and a production issue creates an additional level of pressure. Even in the case of the EuroT program, if there was one big talking point to remember, it was regarding the confidence of handing production support over to London. It was not because of skill or capability gaps but because one needed to resolve issues very quickly. Over the course of several discussions, we reached the conclusion that a small team residing in Bangalore would work on smaller items. But the predominant theme for this team retention was to provide support in case of complex production issues.

The restructuring of teams from feature teams to product-based teams creates additional complexity when solving production issues. With production issues, one may not immediately know which area has been impacted. This fuels a desire to get everyone in on a call. These calls can go in two directions. Either each team will try to "add value" by making suggestions that may not be very relevant to the issue at hand, or they may decide that the discussion is not the best use of their time and will not be engaged in the call. These practices take some time to set in. You can never be too cautious when it comes to production issues. Overheads on communication need to be established before teams reach the new equilibrium. Although a product-based approach ensures deeper technical skills, issues do not necessarily crop up based on Conway's Law. Most production issues require coordination between two or three teams. It could be between the infrastructure and development teams, or perhaps amongst entirely different development teams.

Most releases are followed by patches. Issues that crop up post-release cannot wait for too long. Often, they are not large enough issues to require a full-fledged rerelease. However, each patch needs to be thoroughly validated before it is taken live. Teams often give lesser focus to patches, which may result in the patch creating a larger issue than the one it was trying to fix. When the London team took over, they had a genuine concern regarding patches. New teams may not know the extent of impact with a change. Sometimes the process of a patch release may not be evident. Does a particular patch require a server refresh or will the change take over seamlessly? What type of testing is required and which areas need to be covered? By its very nature, a patch is a short cut. New teams can often end up in two situations. Either they are overly cautious, lengthening the effort involved in the patch. Or decisions they make create further service disruptions. After all, taking a shortcut requires experience.

Production defects also provide a good measure of how well the transition has been going. It's important to know if an issue occurred due to the transition. If so, one needs to do an appropriate root-cause analysis and then fix the problem at the transition level. How quickly one fixes the production issue is a great indicator on the progress that has been made.

DevOps Communication

DevOps has been gaining significant ground as a software development theme. The DevOps model stresses communication and collaboration between developers and IT operations. This is most crucial during the release process and when addressing production defects. The operations members always provide frontline support for production issues. These members reach out to the development teams when they need additional subject matter expertise. In organizations where one has not created an integrated DevOps model, these communications structures are critical. They determine how quickly production issues can get resolved. When an ownership transfer takes place, one needs to proactively redefine these communication channels. Transfer can involve changing the entire development as well as operations or the scope may be limited to either development or operations. Irrespective of the scope, it is of paramount importance to define communication channels. Ensuring smooth camaraderie amongst these groups is even more critical. If the right team spirit is not generated amongst the group, people will hesitate to ask for help. At EuroT, we continued to witness occasions where the operations members reached out to the Bangalore team out of habit. The handover to the new working model took time. But we gave enough time for members to get to know each other and become comfortable with the new working model. We did not encounter issues in resolving production faults. Each interaction afforded the players an opportunity to learn more about the new model of operation.

Costing

Every project within a commercial establishment has one of three objectives: increase revenue, save costs, or meet regulatory requirements. Projects falling within the first two categories need to provide particular focus on costs. The cost of the project cannot go so high that the purpose itself becomes unjustified. Of course, IT costs are only one segment of the overall costs incurred on new initiatives. However, in many cases, they become a significant element. In the case of e-commerce setups, especially in organizations that solely focus on the distribution of assets (such as tickets, music, books) online, IT costs are often the largest. Hence, costing of projects and IT budgets in general is a very important point of discussion.

If ownership transfer occurs within the ambit of outsourcing, then the payment model to the vendor will impact the project. Large service organizations have moved to outcome-based models in order to keep transaction costs low for their customers. In such cases, the cost of projects may be distributed between the development effort and the support timelines. Often, there will be changes to actual rates being charged. Conversely, if a large part of the transition involves insourcing, then employee costs need to be accounted for.

An ownership transfer is replete with changes to processes. As we explored earlier, there are changes to skill sets, the number of teams involved, the approaches to testing, releases, and infrastructure. All of the above impact the way costs are allocated. While it may not always bring down the actual cost, it certainly will impact the method of costing. Accounting for the changes in process, team skills, and structure is far more complex. A new framework that fits in with the new reality needs to be evolved. For example, when more teams are going to be involved, but not on a full-time basis, tracking their time and cost distribution will add to the overheads. If we need to bring in additional layers on project coordination or vendor management, how are these efforts distributed among projects?

Project cost management is a discipline in itself.[5] I cannot cover all facets of this discipline within this book. The key takeaway from this section is to involve the members from the finance and accounting department while the transition is in progress. If you are executing functional projects as part of the transition, you will need their help in budgeting those projects as well. In many instances, the outcome of an ownership transfer would be greater efficiency, which needs to translate into cost savings in some form or the other.

Governance

Governance with respect to IT budgets and projects will change with an ownership transfer. When a new unit takes over, changes may occur around decision flows. In a sense, these reflect the culture of the new unit. They also reflect new reality. The transfer was triggered for a business reason that is projected in the new form of governance. This is especially true with transfers accompanied by structural changes. In the case of EuroT, we made changes to the IT team structure. Whereas one team used to take complete responsibility for delivering a project, multiple teams now had to pitch in. This meant that there were changes to the constitution of the steering committee. The group that directed the project had newer members. The direction from this group had to be followed by a larger set of teams and individuals. Because

---

5. https://en.wikipedia.org/wiki/Project_cost_management

one team had many projects within their fold, a change in direction or priority on one project had to be lined up with the priorities on other projects. A core tenet of project governance is establishing a single point of accountability. This is often lost in the tumult of a transfer. Although the emphasis stays on making the transfer, there isn't enough focus on the structure after the transfer is completed. In a model where multiple teams now execute a project, it is important to define who takes ownership for the project. When the execution structure is consolidated into a single team, the newer model has to be recognized and additional stakeholders need to be taken off of the steering group.

Things to Know and Do

- There will be changes to the way of doing business after ownership transfer. These need to be acknowledged and planned for in advance.

- Team interdependencies will change after the transition.

- There will be changes to the way inceptions are conducted and showcases are done. The constituents in both are bound to change as well.

- Based on the changes to the team structure, additional skill sets may need to be acquired among teams.

- Changes to project execution (with respect to development and testing) can be anticipated. These need to be planned for and facilitated.

- Production support processes will change with the new dispensation. These need to be understood, appreciated, and worked on at the earliest.

- A change in ownership will impact the approach to project costing and the governance structure of projects.

Chapter 12

Measuring Ownership Transfer

By its very nature, software is difficult to measure and value. This perhaps is the reason for the rise of the product mindset within the software field. A product is looked upon from a business angle. This aids decision-makers in putting their dollars in what they consider the right place. The crucial difference, in the case of ownership transfer is the intangibility of the end product. In the case of ownership transfer, no physical product ever appears at the end of the exercise. This transfer is about a new team taking over the workshop that makes the product. In some cases, it is also about shipping the workshop to a different location altogether. Through all of this, the product must not get compromised. The product quality must continue to remain as-is. So how do we measure ownership transfer?

There are two ways to approach measuring ownership transfer. The first and perhaps easier approach is to track the progress on tasks. Create a checklist of the activities to be done or of the knowledge units to be measured and tick them off as each activity is completed. This measures the efficiency of the transfer activity. However, this does not provide a view of the effectiveness of the ownership transfer. As they say, the proof of the pudding is in the eating. The best measure for ownership transfer (and the second way) is in the outcomes that come along with the transfer. There are four broad dimensions to analyze when looking at the transfer outcome. In this chapter we will look at each of these.

Purpose of the Transfer

As with any project, a transfer exercise begins with a project charter, which includes the reason the transfer was initiated in the first place. As mentioned earlier, the transfer could have come about for a number of reasons, including cost, risk mitigation, or vendor consolidation. The steering committee needs to be sure that the teams are progressing in a direction that will meet this purpose. It helps for the steering committee to keep a slide in their presentations outlining the purpose of the program. Time often changes reality. A constant reminder about the purpose of the program allows leadership to strengthen their conviction to the originally stated purpose or to steer the program in a different direction.

Releases

As students, we all had to endure a number of examinations and tests. We studied hard and focused on passing these exams. As children, we may have dreaded those days. At the same time, who can forget that moment of relief, joy, and sheer emptiness of the mind as we left the exam hall? I used to make sure that I was in the best state of mind and health on the days of the exam. All the hard work and preparation would come to nothing if the exam day ended up full of irritants or health issues. Similarly, releases can be like small exams for the team and the product. Successful releases indicate that the team is doing well, the product is progressing in the right direction, and the general health of the system is robust. The metrics of releases during the transfer process give an excellent indication on how well the transfer is going. If the release metrics during the transfer are similar or better than average, then the ownership transfer is going well. If the release metrics show a dip, one must step back and analyze what has gone wrong. It must be kept in mind that releases may not go well for many reasons, so one must not jump to conclusions that the transfer is the only reason for a bad release.

Functional Projects

The purpose of an ownership transfer is to enable the new team to execute projects on their own. The number of functional projects the new team successfully delivers is a strong indicator of the success of the transfer. Two scenarios can play out during or after the transfer. The first, and most common, scenario is that the new team does not get enough functional projects. This is a big risk to the system. Teams need to undertake projects and internalize their skills. The skills under consideration are not just hard skills but experiential skills. Those can be augmented only by getting your hands dirty on the system. If there are no projects to work on, the outcome of the transfer exercise will be poor. Skills of the new team will degrade over time for lack of use. When projects do come up in the future, the team may well be underprepared. In the second scenario, there is a steady stream of functional projects that allow the teams to build up confidence and capability. Here, the teams get to interact with a larger set of stakeholders independently. This allows for the entire organization to settle down into the new status quo. Taking a quick poll with the business stakeholders on their comfort level with the new team is highly recommended at this point.

Incumbent Team Ramp-Down

The size of the incumbent team is a direct indicator of the success of the transfer. If we observe the incumbent team size to be ramping down and the system is none the worse for it, then things are moving in the right direction. It should be noted that this is a metric at the broadest level. You must also examine the profile of the incumbent team as it ramps down. If there is a tendency to retain the most skilled incumbent members for the longest period of time, then the ramp-downs can prove to be a pyrrhic victory. This means that the new team does not have confidence in its skill. As the ramp-downs reach their final phase, decision-making gets tougher. There will be requests to extend the incumbents' tenure. At the extreme, there will be discussions to rebadge skilled incumbent members. Hence, teams will do well to keep an eye on the profile of ramp-downs.

Things to Know and Do

The best way to measure ownership transfer is through outcomes. The following are good measures to track the direction and progress of the transfer:

- Progress toward the purpose of the transfer
- Release metrics
- Health of functional projects in play
- The incumbent team's ramp-down

Chapter 13

The Three Bridges

For decades, knowledge transfers have been limited to a three-month time period, as if that particular timeframe was seared into the collective conscience of IT managers. If the preceding chapters have proven that three months is too short a time to take ownership, the next natural question is, what is the right duration?

Duration of Ownership Transfer

The fact is, there is no one specific timeframe that can be suggested for all ownership transfers. I strongly recommend that a transfer occurs over several releases. To my mind, it should take a minimum of four releases involving both the incumbent and the new teams wherein the new team takes increasingly higher levels of ownership. In the final release, the new team should have taken complete ownership for production support. However, this is not to say that four releases will always suffice. The time period required will also be a function of

- The cultural diversity among teams
- The geographic dispersion
- The complexity of infrastructure transfer

The factors listed above are going to be unique to every team. A platform like EuroT was transferred within a year. The Banker product at Areker was getting customized and transferred over three years. The Arival transition at Creekside took four years before they were able to support all countries. A full rebadging program at MegaTos took eight months. Each of these cases had different types of complexities.

These timelines provide indications of how long it takes for a transfer to complete in its entirety. Aside from that, the new team will need to cross three "bridges" before they get comfortable with the final product. These are the bridges of functionality, skill, and Agile fluency. The longer these bridges are, the greater the time and effort it will take to cross them.

Functionality

The functionality bridge is a familiar one. Most knowledge transfer exercises focus on the purpose of the application, the user flows involved, and the features available as part of the application. Applications built and maintained over long periods will have a number of intrinsic features. For example, consider a simple booking application that has five steps translating into five separate pages. This seems simple enough. However, each field on every page has a story to tell. The length of the field, where the details come from, and to which other system these details relate are vital pieces of information. The way to approach these functional elements is to ask "what" and "why." The "what" refers to the interactions within the system. The "why" speaks to the reason the particular interaction exists in that format. Often, in the rush to complete the transfer, most teams focus only on the "what". The "why" is just as important for the new team to be able to make changes to the application in the future.

At the same time, most teams do not talk about the "why not". What were the alternatives considered and why was one particular approach chosen over others? Some of these questions could be technical, some business-driven, and others might be regulatory. The answers can help in gaining an appreciation of the various constraints within the ecosystem.

Domain Appreciation

In today's world, IT is not just a cost center. It is often a point of competitive advantage; an enabler for the organization to move ahead. Therefore, the new team should have a good appreciation of that industry. It allows the group not just to take orders from business, but also to work as partners in the move to create systems of differentiation. You can find the word *innovation* in virtually every company's mission, vision, or value statements. In a world where organizations are looking to create a differentiated experience for their customers, IT and its applications deliver that unique value.

On closer inspection, it's easy to see that these experiences of differentiation are nothing but unique functionalities delivered using cutting-edge technologies or just unique features backed by smart thinking. Understanding user preferences and the evolving nature of customer aspirations play a key role in determining these experiences of differentiation.

It can make a difference when a new team comes in with a good understanding of the industry norms. Business jargon and acronyms are always being thrown around. Many industries have strong business rules and regulations to comply with. For the healthcare sector, it's HIPAA. In the case of finance, entire subjects, such as maintaining a balance sheet, must be read up on. There are industry standards to determine nonperforming assets or calculate insurance premiums, and even country-specific rules on security transactions. In the realm of travel, you can often get confused about the difference between a journey leg, a journey segment, and a travel sector. The less a team understands the industry, the longer it will take for them to come up to speed. A poor understanding of the industry will also be a deterrent for the team to ask the right questions at the time of the hand over. The "why not" questions may be misplaced if the new team comes in with less industry experience.

Cross-Domain Experience

At the same time, there are many opportunities for people to adapt practices used in other industries. Many best practices cross-pollinate, especially in the e-commerce world. A regular user wants a level of familiarity when traversing the Web. If the user is, say, transferring money to her parents, booking a train ticket for her family, or purchasing a coveted accessory online, she would expect that these transactions would all follow similar interactions and provide similar security standards. Hence, domain must not be construed to be just practices followed within one specific industry. New teams need to keep an open mind when picking up practices from other industries. This can often be a bonus with an ownership transfer. A new team can bring in a fresh perspective.

I was part of a team that worked on redesigning the website for a large airline. Almost all of the work centered on user experience. We had flown in people from across the world for this exercise. However, as things progressed, the timelines on the project shifted, and the original members could not continue with the project because of other commitments. We had to bring in new members to take over. The biggest challenge faced by the new members was the lack of domain understanding. Not having the time to learn the industry while working on the designs hurt us a lot.

The greater the gap between functionality and domain, the longer the effort to take ownership will be. Teams need to make an initial investment of acquiring domain knowledge and understanding. This could mean either bringing in members with relevant domain expertise or investing time in training. It helps to obtain domain appreciation before diving deep into an ownership transfer exercise.

Being a User

Knowing what the end customer wants is critical. If we are working on a retail website, for example, it would help us to have shopped online at least once. This would give us insight as to how things need to flow. An IT department that understands the business's end customer can truly function both as a consultant and as a partner in the business. On business-to-business or highly device-centric products such as flight cockpit applications, the development team may not have direct experience in utilizing the application. In such cases, the new team should address the limitations upfront and explore opportunities toward understanding the business layout. Some time back, I worked with a team that developed the baggage management system for a large airline product company. As IT professionals, we often do not get the opportunity to use this system. The application is used by airport supervisors, baggage handlers, and airline agents to facilitate smooth bag transfers. At the team's request, we arranged a trip to the Bengaluru airport where an earlier version of this product was deployed. The team obtained access to the baggage handling section from the appropriate authorities, and we witnessed how the system is currently used. The baggage handler needed to scan each bag before putting it in the container. We experienced firsthand what the implications were of a slow response. Thousands of bags needed to be loaded. A one-second delay in response could quickly add up to over thousands of bags. This could delay the departure of flights and, in the case of transfers, cause bags to miss the flight. We also received critical insight as to how the handlers used their scan machines, as well as what usage scenarios were critical for the supervisors. For example, we noticed that when loading, the handlers would scan each bag and then put it up into the container. However when unloading, they would pull out all bags at one time. When all the bags were down, they proceeded to scan each bag on the ground. Understanding this could make a huge impact when it comes to taking ownership. Now, our team was not just reliant on what the product owner said. They truly understood how the application was put to use.

Skill

The skill bridge is quite visible. In fact, most IT service organizations categorize the members of their workforce based on technology and skill, for example, a member may be known as a Java person, a .Net person, or a SAP professional. When a new project comes up, the request to the operations team goes out expressed in terms of the number of developers, testers, and BAs required. The next level of detail concerns the type of technology experience required—does he understand J2EE?; which (or how many) application servers is he conversant with?; and how many years of experience does he have?

Program managers articulate the complexity of an exercise by the number of people involved and the kind of technical expertise required. The more diverse the skill set, the greater the complexity of the project. To a large extent, this makes sense. One typically needs a doctor to replace another doctor or a surgeon to take over from another surgeon. However, technical skill goes beyond just having experience in Java or Scala. Appreciating and adopting engineering processes are technical skills as well. Following test-driven development requires skill. Unlike hardcore language skills, some of these skills are "a moment to learn, a lifetime to master" types of skills. Running build systems and supporting the platform that runs the development and test environments requires skill. DevOps skills needed to run large platforms are equally dear when taking over projects in Agile environments. Quite often, these skills are not identified upfront as key requirements.

Contextual Ambidexterity

As organizations are in various stages of Agile adoption, team members are faced with the need to demonstrate contextual ambidexterity.[1] *Contextual ambidexterity* is a unique skill that describes a team member's ability to balance between aligning to an organization's strictures and adapting to fluid on-ground situations. For example, some developers may be required to align with quality control metrics on the one hand, and at the same time they may need to don a tester's hat to help complete a story.

---

1. https://www.london.edu/faculty-and-research/lbsr/organisational-ambidexterity#.VuFFH5N97BI

Quality Analysis Skills

Testing brings in its own unique set of challenges. Testing skills are often overlooked when large programs are charted out. In this day and age, many different kinds of technologies are involved in testing. From unit tests, to service tests, integration tests, and functional tests, there are various tools and technologies used for building and running automation tests. Quality analysts need to possess the skills to run these types of tests. Gone are the days when you could use bug-tracking tools to log defects and utilize complex Excel spreadsheets to present test reports. Today's environments require strong automation suites that run almost continuously in order to support continuous deployment. Within the ambit of technical skills, you need to factor for testing skills as well.

Skill for the Future

Leadership expects a transition to bring improvements. Improvements will not occur if the new team continues to do exactly the same things the old team did. Viewing the existing landscape as a reference for the skill sets you will need in the future is a rather myopic view. The new team ought to acquire the skill sets that create the future. This calls for a deeper appreciation of the expectations from the engagement. During the early days of Agile adoption, we often simplified Agile projects to a set of tasks such as stand-ups and retrospectives. These were accompanied with new metric models involving velocities and burn-down charts. Together, these defined the processes in the Agile journey. The next evolution in this journey is on the platform. Build systems, test automation, and virtual environments are platforms on which the Agile journey moves along. This is where real monetary investments need to be made. One important component of that investment is in skills. The team that drives this journey needs to be proficient with these skills. The regular models of maintenance are changing rapidly. Automation is creeping in. DevOps is gaining acceptance as a delivery model. If these skill sets are not readily available for the new team, the outcomes from the transition will take much longer than expected.

Agile Fluency

Agile fluency has been a hidden bridge for some time now.[2] Diana Larsen and James Shore coined this term in 2012. Their model provides four evolutionary stages that Agile teams go through. In the first stage, teams focus on value and eliminating

---

2. http://martinfowler.com/articles/agileFluency.html

waste. These teams (identified as one-star teams by the authors) break up requirements from a business perspective. These typically take the form of user stories. These teams also report progress from a business perspective.

In the second stage, teams begin to deliver value based on market cadence. These teams do everything that the one-star teams do, but they also create and manage software so that they can ship whenever the market demands. This stage is perhaps the most difficult stage to master, because it calls for significant skill improvements for each team member. Although the first stage involves management reorientation and soft skills, the second stage requires significant hard skill acquisition. These skills range from test automation and continuous integration to test-driven development. These engineering practices are essential to delivering low-defect software and are the key to delivering software on market cadence.

At the three-star stage, teams are able to partner effectively with business to optimize the value delivered. Often, product management personnel are embedded within the teams. The lines between software metrics and business metrics have a tendency to blur within these teams. Combining their one- and two-star skills, the team produces features to bring in maximum value. They do this by using several Agile and Lean techniques, actualizing innovation, taking it quickly to the market, and obtaining validated feedbacks.

Four-star teams operate at a level where their practices and outcomes impact the whole enterprise. These teams are able to view the complete enterprise as a single system and to optimize value for the system. There are very few cases of teams operating at a four-star level.

Teams Operating at Different Levels

Although we distinguish four different levels of Agile fluency, in my mind, the model is really more of a continuum. Teams operate at different levels within this space. In large enterprises, most Agile teams operate between the one- and two-star stages. As a new team takes over, the level at which this team operates compared to the incumbent will have a bearing on the effort involved. A team operating at a lower fluency will take much longer to achieve stability. The members will need to reorient their daily operations as well as their interactions to measure up to a higher star. Teams can sometimes take at least three months of deliberate practice to settle in the right fluency. If the differences are on skill sets, it can take much longer.

A team operating at a higher level of fluency may bring in change conflicts within the program. This is not necessarily a bad thing. Often, transformational change is required to improve an organization's efficiency. Many of our engagements at ThoughtWorks involve enabling IT teams to operate at higher points of Agile fluency. One such engagement involved us working together with the client's team on delivering a critical project. The client also wanted us to inculcate sound Agile practices amongst their teams. The client personnel soon realized that most activities we picked up for development were taking much longer than they had expected. Because we had stringent timelines to meet, this made the client restless. In their minds, we were taking too long. It takes time to pull the teams into practicing a different set of coding practices. After new techniques, such as test-driven development and pair programming, are introduced, the teams may see a dip in productivity. Most ThoughtWorks developers felt that they could not write code without writing test cases first. In this particular example, after test cases were written and integrated to the build, these test cases started failing. Failure often occurred because the external services that the module interacted with were flaky (meaning the external services would often fail). Often, our client managers got frustrated with our need to write test cases. From their point of view, we ought to accept that the services were flaky, so it was a waste of time to have written these automated tests in the first place. But those tests were really challenging the status quo. A classic case of change conflict. Over time, we exerted enough influence to stabilize these external services as well.

When Higher Agile Fluency Becomes a Problem

Amacle is one the largest IT product companies in the world, with revenues of more than US $30 billion. They grew rapidly through acquisitions, and in 2005 they picked up an identity management company, Obelicks. These were the early days of Agile, and this organization could not match the speed at which Obelicks was putting features into production. Obelicks released features into production every week, whereas Amacle's management group were used to releasing every twelve weeks. So, in effect, Amacle had to get Obelicks to slow down their releases. In this case, the larger and the more dominant organization decided to bring Agile fluency down to what suited their world.

Pairing elicits a very similar debate. One of the biggest excuses from our client personnel is that there isn't enough time for pairing. Pairing and pair switch ensures that many eyes look at the same piece of code. This naturally brings in the review element. The initial rounds of pairing are learning experiences because team members get acclimatized to the new way of working. Efficiency will get worse before it gets better.

The status quo demands delivery within constraints. Transformation looks to remove constraints. A new team arriving at a lower fluency level will face the same challenge as an organization engaging a higher fluency team to take ownership for its software. Both cases involve transformation at some level.

Things to Know and Do

- Duration of ownership transfer should occur across releases.

- Duration can depend upon cultural differences, geographic spread, and infrastructure scope.

- The new team will need to cross the three bridges of functionality, skill, and Agile fluency in order to fully take over. Duration and difficulty of the transfer depends on how long these bridges are.

- In today's Agile paradigm, one needs to account for testing skills as well as a level of contextual ambidexterity within the new team.

Chapter 14

Putting It Together

An ownership transfer exercise is a layered program. It needs to be viewed through two lenses: one focusing on execution and the other on change management.

The previous chapters talk about the implementation phase of the ownership transfer. Figure 14.1 provides a single view of the many different nodes to consider in this form of exercise.

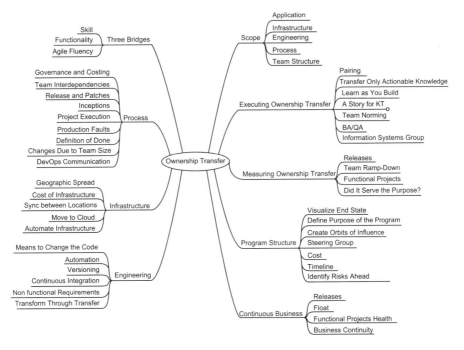

Figure 14.1 *Mind map—ownership transfer*

Change Management

An ownership transfer is a change management exercise as well. Some changes are subtle, and some are not. Many unstated expectations may only come out during moments of frustration. As with the example of a new baby, one cannot slowly ease into taking care of the baby. If she is crying, she needs to be fed. If the diapers are soiled, they need to be changed. There is no waiting period there.

Thankfully, with IT applications, you have the opportunity to take over at a slower pace. Even so, it helps to know what changes to expect through the transfer and after its completion. Jason Little's *Lean Change Management* is a great book to read for more insight on this subject.[1] In an ownership transfer exercise, you can expect change to occur across four levels: Individual, Team, Organization, and at the Global level. Please refer to Figure 14.2.

Figure 14.2 *Change management—ownership transfer*

Individual

At the most granular level, an ownership transfer exercise impacts every individual within the team. It challenges the status quo for the person and ushers changes in multiple dimensions.

Reskilling

Mahendra Singh Dhoni has been the most successful Indian cricket team captain. India won several trophies including the One-Day International World Cup and the T20 World Cup under his captaincy. He started off as a swashbuckling batsman, hitting bowlers all around the park without a care in the world. As he matured and

---

1. www.amazon.com/Lean-Change-Managment-Innovative-Organizational/dp/0990466507/ref=sr_1_1?
ie=UTF8&qid=1448518622&sr=8-1&keywords=lean+change+management

was given the captaincy of the team, he retooled his game to help the team win more games. He transformed from someone scoring runs at a rapid pace while taking risks, to someone who can be relied on to play through to the end and win games. He had to reskill his game to suit the new reality.

Similarly, an employee needs to adjust how they work and learn new skills during an ownership transfer exercise. *Skill* is the ability to do a task well. Skills develop only through active participation, developing stories, and fixing defects. It's important to have an open mind to learn new things, as well as to let go of old habits. Dhoni did not become the great finisher that he is overnight. He applied himself game after game, defended balls that he would have earlier thrashed until the match came down to the wire.

Recalibrating Expectations

Every assignment brings with it new experiences, new colleagues, and new expectations. As we grow in the corporate world, we can appreciate how career-limiting it is to rest on our laurels. The same holds true with ownership transfer. Expectations are recalibrated through the exercise. During the pairing phase, there is always an incumbent member to look up to and lean upon when faced with daunting decisions. As time goes by, the new team member needs to step up and make those decisions himself. The team member needs to accept that this truly is his baby.

Team Interactions

Pairing with others can sometimes bring in extreme experiences. Pairing with the right person can be a resounding high. On the other hand, pairing with a difficult person can suck the energy out of a person's day. Teams may be merged or redistributed, which forces individuals to work with people they might have not worked with earlier. A person's social side will be tested throughout this exercise. Some people thrive in these situations, whereas others develop a deathly pallor at the thought of meeting new people. It's never easy to change one's social personality. However, it can be helpful to be forewarned about any impending changes that might be coming to a team.

Team

Teams go through changes in their makeup and character as well during an ownership transfer.

Resistance to Change

Resistance to change is perhaps one of the biggest challenges of an ownership transfer program. Especially in an Agile context where employees identify with their teams strongly, this resistance can manifest throughout the entire unit. Original teams will unravel in this program. As individuals from the incumbent and the new team pair, existing teams will morph. As the transfer moves into the process side of things, restructuring is inevitable. The composition and skill sets within teams will undergo change. Change management particularly impacts team dynamics.

As individuals, we all have our unique points of view. Seldom will we witness situations where all team members agree on a topic. But strong team bonding ensures members will back each other up. The "not invented here" syndrome (discussed in Chapter 6 on culture) is a classic case in which one team member can influence the entire unit to take adverse positions. Similarly, as the new team takes over from the incumbent, there will be strong resistance to pick up the "baggage" of the old team.

Team Restructure

Teams will be in flux throughout the duration of a transition. As we moved through our own transfer in EuroT, the Bangalore teams had London members joining in and vice versa. On the flipside, as Bangalore ramped down, some of those teams were merged. These shake-ups can take a toll on the social infrastructure of the program. For many employees, a team is like a second home. You feel at home with your team. You are bound to feel disoriented when that home keeps changing. A room suddenly disappears and another comes up in a different place. A new person joins your home and an old person leaves. It may not feel like home anymore!

Ownership transfer can also bring together teams that have not interacted before. Culture clashes amongst teams can slow progress. Leadership would do well to amplify team norming and forming activities to preempt such situations.

Organization

The 2004 Indian Ocean earthquake occurred on 26th of December off the coast of Sumatra. It occurred in the morning around 7:58 AM local time. Most people in Africa and the Indian subcontinents were asleep at that time, blissfully unaware of the approaching danger. Within a few hours, the resultant tsunamis wreaked havoc thousands of kilometers away in dozens of countries. More than two hundred and fifty thousand people lost their lives. A tectonic event in one part of the world created a massive impact on places thousands of kilometers away.

In a similar vein, though at a much smaller scale and of course without the accompanying adversities, an ownership transfer in one part of the company brings in waves that impact all other parts of the organization. These waves will wash over every orbit of influence. As they move further away from the epicenter, their impact will lessen.

Wide Impact

Modern day organizations are making structural as well as physical changes to the way IT interacts with business. These days, IT team members often sit along with business groups, in order to enable seamless communications. Changes to these IT and IS teams impact daily interactions with business. New vendor personnel will bring their practices and thought processes into the mix.

Groups one or two steps removed from an ownership transfer exercise will likely have a superficial appreciation of the purpose of the transfer. These groups can form misplaced opinions and pass denigrating judgments on the progress of this exercise. Ownership transfer can become the fall guy for every failure within an organization, no matter how large or small. This is true not just of ownership transfer, but of any change management program. Leadership teams need to keep a close eye on the exercise and shield it from adverse influences. Steering groups of such an exercise must have cross-sectional representation across departments. Department heads need to be informed and invested towards the success of the transfer.

Outsourcing

In outsourcing situations, as more of the work is handed over to the vendor, the internal teams will likely begin to feel a loss of control. People who started off "teaching" the newbies, eventually find themselves shunted out of the classroom. This loss of control can be very difficult to handle. This sentiment will also exist with incumbent teams, irrespective of the type of transfer. In the case of client-to-vendor transfers, these sentiments will be amplified, because a loss of control might be accompanied with an enhanced sense of insecurity.

Global Village

They say the sun never sets on the British Empire in the 19th and early 20th Centuries. This period witnessed the Portuguese, French, and the British aggressively exploring and annexing vast territories to their empires. However, once annexed, these territories were treated very differently from the mainland. Little attention was paid to the welfare of the people in the territories they had acquired. Indeed, these territories were treated as though they existed only to satiate the growing needs of the mainland.

In the late 1990s, organizations spread out to low-cost destinations in order to take advantage of the cost arbitrage. Global connectivity and the Internet helped substantially bridge the communication divide. Two decades later, organizations continue to offshore, but the need has moved on from mere cost arbitrage to acquiring the right talent and processes. Yet some organizations still treat their offshore counterparts in much the same way the British Empire dealt with their colonies.

National Culture

At some deep level, cultural prejudices amongst nations continue to reverberate in daily operations. Quite often, we do not understand how things work in the other land.

Geert Hofstede has provided a good framework to appreciate national cultures.[2]

- *Individualism vs collectivism.* Nations such as the United States emphasize individualism whereas others like Japan focus on the collective group.

- *Power distance.* Cultures that favor collectivism show a tendency to have greater power distance. Power distance is the measure of unequal power distribution in an organization.

- *Uncertainty avoidance.* This is the notion of risk appetites among people of a nation. A low risk-taking populace, such as the people of Greece, prefer predictability and security. Low uncertainty avoidance countries are more entrepreneurial in nature.

- *Masculinity vs femininity.* Traditionally masculine cultures see a dominance of "tough" values such as achievement, material success, and competition. More feminine cultures lay greater emphasis upon personal relationships, quality of life, and employee well-being.

People brought up in different nations are predisposed to reflect their national culture. In situations where ownership transfer occurs over geographies, these value conflicts will come to the fore.

Communication is another key attribute over distributed development. Most people think in their mother tongue. When distributed development occurs across

---

2. http://geert-hofstede.com/national-culture.html

nations that do not share a common language, this facet comes in the way. It takes a little extra effort for people to translate their thoughts into a common medium for communication. This additional effort inhibits free communication. People are often searching for the right word, term, or tense. This can break a person's train of thought and the essence gets compromised. In a sense, people do not convey everything that is on their mind.

Things to Know and Do

- Ownership transfer is a layered program with execution elements and change management elements.
- Managing change is highly crucial in ownership transfer,
- Change can occur at four levels, Individual, Team, Organization, and at a Global Level.

Chapter 15

Conclusion

In 2011, I interviewed a candidate for a possible developer role in my company. She had about three years of experience. I found her knowledge and approach to be good. As is wont, I started asking some questions about software development processes. Imagine my surprise when she said that she did not know the traditional SDLC (software development life cycle). She had worked only on Agile projects. This was an epiphany of sorts for me. We now live in a world in which some software professionals start their careers only on Agile projects.

The Lean Agile March

Ten years from now, most of the Fortune 1000 organizations will have either adopted Agile or conducted significant pilots on Agile delivery models. Some of these companies will have likely honed their Agile practices to impact the entire organization. Upstream businesses may have added Lean principles and systems thinking on to Agile practices as well. In effect, one can expect further refinements and evolution in the Lean Agile process of software development. We can also expect these concepts to impact operations of the larger organization.

This may be a good point for us to remind ourselves of the Agile Manifesto[1]

- Individuals and interactions over processes and tools
- Working software over comprehensive documentation
- Customer collaboration over contract negotiation
- Responding to change over following a plan

---

1. www.agilemanifesto.org/

The second point of the manifesto talks about working software over comprehensive documentation. However, most knowledge transfer exercises today still follow the traditional route of evaluation, process study, and transition activity. Most of these activities are completed within three months, with half this time focused on planning. The new team doesn't get enough opportunities to work on the system. Teams undertake activities of shadowing and reverse shadowing for a period of under two months. A lot of focus is further laid on documentation. Many IT service organizations put tremendous focus on documenting the application maintenance process as part of the transition. In the Agile paradigm, this focus is viewed as misplaced. Many of us have been part of software and maintenance teams. When managing system-critical applications, I have encountered several production issues. I do not recollect any instance where any of us went back to refer to documentation when a high priority issue hit us. We called up people, discussed things over conference calls, reached out to former team members, and tried to bring experts into the exercise. Imagine if you visited a doctor and she pulled out a reference book to make her diagnosis. Your trust in that doctor would come crashing down. When faced with production issues, one expects people to know what to do. This comes with practice and experience, not through documentation.

Many of my colleagues in the IT space have spoken about the kind of effort it requires to take over critical applications. One such instance involved taking over more than four hundred and fifty applications, originally operated by the customer personnel. The handover was officially completed in three months. They found that not all applications were critical and some were minor forms that found little use. Even then, four hundred and fifty is a very large number of applications to be transitioned in such a short amount of time. When I pressed him about how they were able to carry on such a huge exercise in such a short time, he recalled the heroism required in running the system after the three-month period. Expectedly, production tickets doubled and ticket resolution time increased. The new team had to find their way around. He admitted that things only began to stabilize after a year of high effort and stress. Heroes are born when we place unreal expectations on people and teams. But the purpose of the IT organization is not to create heroes. IT organizations exist to provide consistent value. Processes exist to ensure a level of consistency in that value. However, if processes are defined without an understanding of the daily realities of the organization, delivering on expectations will require super-human effort. The customer CIO carried the risk of this large exercise. If this project had failed, he would have lost his job. This again begs the question about setting unrealistic expectations. True takeover can be defined as complete only when the new setup begins to provide the same level of stability, if not better, compared to the prior group.

Whenever someone is asked to take over an application, there is also an expectation that there will be an improvement in the process of developing and releasing software. This expectation is bound to exist with all transfer activities. After all, the purpose of the transition is improvement in some form. This effectively means that we cannot rest on just maintaining status quo. Imagine a scenario where the current organization has become agile. When the new setup takes over, the minimum expectation is for the new group to adopt the same level of agile competence. This calls for organizations to appreciate Agile concepts from a development and maintenance perspective.

Incentives

The practical challenge with this approach of ownership transfer is about keeping the incumbent motivated through the exercise. This is a tough leadership challenge. An ownership transfer could be construed as a negative mark on the incumbent's performance. The leadership needs to set the right tone for this exercise. In some instances, it could be a case of build, operate, transfer (BOT), a logical move from the incumbent to the new team. In other instances, it can be more of a transformation exercise than just a transition activity. Every member in that group is creating the future. The new team will be living with that future, and the incumbents will move on to create the future in another place. That perspective provides a vastly different motivation for everybody involved. Each team member brings value to the exercise. If those members are provided with autonomy and purpose, they will inevitably be motivated to work toward a successful transfer. Daniel Pink's book, *Drive: The Surprising Truth About What Motivates Us*[2] is an excellent reference on motivation and drive.

At the same time, there is the perspective of the management personnel from the incumbent's side, for whom intrinsic motivation would not be relevant. These members are not directly working on the transition. Their intent would be to either expand their business (in the case of vendors) or pursue their unit goals. Offering or extending some of their key staff for the transfer exercise would not necessarily help their own professional interests. In this case, the IT leadership should try and create an incentive program for the incumbent. Incentives can be tied to success a year or two after the program has run its course. These rewards can be linked to three of the dimensions used to track ownership transfer (chapter 12):

- Tracking the release metrics
- Tracking the functional projects
- Meeting the purpose of the transfer

---

2. www.amazon.com/Drive-Surprising-Truth-About-Motivates/dp/1594484805

This helps ensure alignment among the management of the incumbents. Incumbents will be more amenable to putting their skin in the game. It also moves the dialogue from one of penalization to one of partnership.

Start Early

A core (but often unspoken) tenet in this book is about starting early. In several places, I elaborated on the need to plan the transition for a longer duration. Starting early and planning for a longer duration are, in many ways, two sides of the same coin. In the case of transitions, management often spends enormous time discussing, debating, and then recovering from analysis fatigue. Quite often, the trigger for action could be one incident that creates the proverbial tipping point. Instead, if management decides to move into the transition early with an open mindset, it creates further models, options, and perspectives to make clearer decisions. It does not cost a lot to start early. On the other hand, there is a lot to benefit by identifying risks earlier and in general gaining a better perspective on things. After all, one cannot learn to swim sitting in a classroom.

Sign-Off

By now, we should appreciate that ownership transfers are extremely complex exercises involving several teams, partners, departments, and vendors. Different stakeholders will come in with their own motivations and incentives. Applying Theory X[3], as developed by Douglas McGregor, will not yield benefits. Theory X, in short, propounds that employees on the whole dislike work. Hence, they need to be instructed, forced, and micro-managed. Theory Y, on the other hand, encourages creating the right working environment that motivates employees to perform. At the same time, in the case of ownership transfer, not all parties are so invested that Theory Y in itself would also succeed. We need to find a good balance between these two approaches. We must plan in advance, but at the same time, we must be open to adapting our plans. The benefits of doing so are immense. In fact, a transfer executed over the long term will not fail. It offers enough opportunities to see what is working and what is not. The longer timeframe also allows enough opportunities to clarify our assumptions and unearth the unknowns. In the most dramatic of situations, we may realize that our original structure is actually better than the newly envisaged one. If we realize this, it gives us the opportunity to change direction.

---

3. www.businessballs.com/mcgregor.htm

All of this may sound inconvenient at first blush. But that inconvenience is mostly in our minds. Go ahead, give it a shot!

Things to Know and Do

- Most IT professionals will only know the Agile way of working in another ten years. Ownership transfer needs to align with the Agile philosophy as well.

- Transformation always accompanies an ownership transfer. The team is creating the future.

- Leadership must plan for practical incentives to keep the incumbent engaged in the program.

- Branding the program as one of transformation provides a larger purpose to the incumbent staff on the ground.

- Outcome-linked and time-based incentives may ensure the incumbent management remains invested in the transfer.

Chapter 16

Epilogue

The journey at EuroT did not stop with the transformation program. The team recognized there were further summits to climb. The program originally focused on the IT organization. The next step was to move the larger organization toward the Agile path. As always, the change had to occur in the mind first. You can never "do Agile." You can only "be Agile." The leadership at EuroT deeply appreciated this subtle but profound notion. After the IT restructure, EuroT then looked to perform the same exercise at an organizational level. In the earlier scenario, we had nine different teams working on almost every project. This was not working out so well. It was becoming a nine-legged race. More importantly, the relationship between the commercial and technical teams had become those of a client and supplier. The development teams used to look upon the commercial teams as their customer.

The EuroT leadership decided to reorganize some of the teams into clusters, broadly defined as groups speaking to specific customer segments. One cluster was assembled to focus on systems interacting with industry data (data from centralized systems in the European travel industry). Simultaneously, and perhaps more importantly, each cluster was made up of both business and technical team members. Each of the clusters had a business stakeholder; a senior executive who guided the cluster for their two-to-three year roadmap. Each cluster also had a dedicated product owner. Before this, the product owner would identify more with the business group and would work with any of the project teams. Now, she identified herself either with cluster A or cluster B. From a client-vendor relationship, the IT and business groups became a single team.

The product owner was given the responsibility to come up with the roadmap for his cluster. This roadmap had both a functional and a technical element. Technical elements could range from the usage of micro services to automated service tests, or even moving to the cloud. The entire team, comprising the business and technical folks, worked together to define the product roadmap. The IT and business teams transitioned from a client-supplier relationship to a single team with a common purpose. Ownership for the product grew by several notches.

Product ownership translated into a deeper understanding of the domain for the team. Because the team members had worked with the product for a longer period of time, there was continuity in their decisions. This led to greater integrity of the product vision. Design decisions are made keeping the product roadmap in mind, not just to satisfy the next urgent project need.

Each product cluster owned their architecture. In real-world terms, this meant that each product cluster could decide if and when they would move to the cloud. They drove their design, build, test, and deploy processes. Systems had been decoupled to provide a fair level of autonomy during the transformation program itself. The product clusters were able to determine the frequency of their releases to production as well as their path toward continuous delivery. Of course, the cluster groups still needed to ensure that their vision and operations were congruent with the enterprise's vision.

Organizational restructuring was also accompanied with budget realignment. In the past, budgets were allocated for specific projects. The challenge with a project-centric budget had been the stop/start approach to projects and a general compromise toward the technical stability of the product. Stakeholders were happy so long as the feature was made available. Resolving technical debts became a distant priority. The budgeting process was realigned so each cluster received its own budget. The overall process was now more aligned to the product vision. The cluster teams now had more of a say in making the products stronger and more stable for the future.

Some clusters also added a couple of operations members. These members were the first line of defense for production issues. With this, the clusters became truly cross-functional. They were enabled and empowered to take ideas from concept to cash. Each cluster now represented a cross-section of the organization.

In the new set-up, the development teams would ask the product owner of the business model for a new feature, the ROI (return on investment) on a project, and the reasons why the new feature ought to be prioritized over another. The developers also provided data-driven inputs to the business teams and provided suggestions on which features stood a greater chance of adoption. The developers provided substantial value and suggestions on user experience as well.

Some of EuroT's business is from building and supporting platforms for other bus and train companies. Earlier interactions with these companies were limited to the product owner and the account manager. In the new scheme of things, personnel from these companies interacted directly with the EuroT technical teams. A higher sense of ownership amongst team members had developed. Clearly this team was marching toward three stars on the Agile fluency framework.

On the engineering side, the clusters continued to evolve their delivery mechanism. Freed of the monolith's shackles, each product cluster rapidly defined their path toward greater product-centricity and continuous delivery. This also created healthy competition amongst different clusters. Today, many modules make two to three releases in a week, while retaining the ability for backwards compatibility. Even as interdependencies exist amongst clusters, each cluster is able to develop and release on their own.

During the early days of the program, a release involved a down time of five hours. Downtimes are now less than fifteen minutes. In the past, releases were major events whose outcome the entire organization would await with bated breath. Releases were once done every three months; this was slowly brought down to five-week cycles. Before every release, the team spent an enormous amount of time testing the stability of the rollback process. Now, many releases occur in a week. Blue Green deployments[1] eliminate the need to undertake a dedicated rollback activity before every release. As part of the release process, all of the production machines are regularly torn down and rebuilt. The automation of virtual machines conceived and built during the transformation program is finally paying rich dividends.

The team's next destination is to completely move to the cloud and to simultaneously mature their continuous delivery. To think that it all started with what most would call a knowledge transfer!

---

1. http://martinfowler.com/bliki/BlueGreenDeployment.html

Bibliography

Adler, Nancy. *International Dimensions of Organisational Behavior*, 5th edition, South-Western College Pub, 2007.

Allworth, James, Karen Dillon, and Clayton M. Christensen. *How Will You Measure Your Life*, HarperCollins, 2012.

Barrett, Frank J. *Yes to the Mess—Surprising Leadership Lessons from Jazz*, Harvard Business Review Press, 2012.

Gladwell, Malcolm. *Outliers—The Story of Success*, Back Bay Books, 2009.

Iyengar, Sheena. *The Art of Choosing*, Reprint edition, Twelve, 2011.

Little, Jason. *Lean Change Management*, 2nd edition, Happy Melly Express, 2014.

Pink, Daniel. *Drive: The Surprising Truth About What Motivates Us*, Canongate Books, 2010.

Razeghi, Andrew. *The Riddle—Where Ideas Come from and How To Have Better Ones*, Jossey-Bass, 2008.

Ries, Eric. *The Lean Startup: How Today's Entrepreneurs Use Continuous Innovation to Create Radically Successful Businesses*, 1st edition, Crown Business, 2011.

Schumpeter, Joseph A. *Capitalism Socialism and Democracy*, Harper Perennial Modern Classics, 1950.

Glossary

Agile—In the context of this book, this is used to refer to a mindset that is aligned with the values and principles outlined in the Agile Manifesto. It is not used in the sense of the common English adjective.

Agile fluency—Agile fluency is determined by the way a team develops and releases software when it is under pressure (or is distracted). It describes the degree to which Agile practices have been internalized by the team.

Agile organization—For the purposes of this book, an Agile organization is one that is quick to respond to changes in the marketplace. This organization responds positively to rapidly changing environments. Such organizations typically have a flat structure and their employees are highly empowered.

automation—The act of replacing routine manual tasks using machines.

change conflict—Conflicts arising out of organizational change programs.

change management—A systematic approach to ensuring changes are thoroughly and effectively implemented. There are three broad aspects to change management: adapting to change, dealing with change, and making the change.

continuous delivery (CD)—An approach to delivering software that is frequent and uneventful. This is achieved through seamless automation from development to deployment.

continuous integration—A practice followed by software development teams of frequently checking code into a version control system, which then automatically triggers a suite of fast-running tests. Continuous integration ensures that the codebase retains its functional integrity in the face of rapid development.

COTS (commercial off-the-shelf products)—In the context of this book, COTS refers to software products that are bought off the shelf and implemented.

cross-functional team—A team comprised of people with inter-disciplinary skills who work together to realize an outcome.

DevOps—The combination of development and operations staff, which aims to improve collaboration between the development organization and IT-operations by locating these skills within a single team and by emphasizing culture, automation, measurement, and sharing.

inception—The starting point of a new activity. In the context of this book, inception is a definition exercise that sets the stage for a project and creates an initial backlog of activities.

incumbent—A person or a team who currently holds responsibility for the application.

ISV (independent software vendor)—Including vendors recently categorized as software-as-a-service company. Examples include Salesforce, GitHub.

iteration—In the context of the Agile methodology, a timebox within which project activities occur. A project is typically broken down into iterations of equal duration. Iterations normally range from one to four weeks. Of late a majority of teams are defining iterations of two weeks.

ITIL (Information Technology Infrastructure Library)—A set of practices for IT service management that tries to align IT services with the needs of business.

ITSM (IT service management)—The sum total of policies, processes, and procedures that come together to provide IT services to an organization. ITSM takes a process-centric approach toward management.

KT (knowledge transfer)—The practical aspect of transferring knowledge from one part of an organization to another.

outcome-oriented team—A team that is empowered and accountable for an outcome (such as, for example, a cross-functional product team).

power distance—Power Distance refers to the way power is distributed. In particular, it is a measure of the extent to which the less powerful accept and expect that power is distributed unequally.

product—In the context of this book, a computer program that satisfies a want or need.

rebadging—The process of transitioning employees of one company to become employees of a second company. The affected personnel continue to provide services to the first company. However, they now work as vendor personnel and not as full-time employees.

retrospective—In the context of this book, a meeting that's held at the end of an iteration. During the retrospective, the team reflects on what happened during the iteration and identifies ways to improve processes for the next iteration.

risk—An uncertain event, which, if it occurs, has an impact on the outcome of the project. Normally risk takes on a negative connotation. But a risk can be an event that has a positive impact on the project as well.

SLA (service-level agreement)—Part of a standardized contract in which different levels of services are formally defined. In the context of this book, SLAs broadly define the speed and type of response for issues of varying severities.

smoke test—Preliminary tests that check for defects so basic that if they exist the prospective release may need to be rejected.

TP (transformation program)—In the context of the hypothetical EuroT organization, a program that looks to support the EuroT IT program with two-fifths of the original capacity of the program.

Index

REGISTER YOUR PRODUCT at informit.com/register

Access Additional Benefits and SAVE 35% on Your Next Purchase

- Download available product updates.

- Access bonus material when applicable.

- Receive exclusive offers on new editions and related products.
  (Just check the box to hear from us when setting up your account.)

- Get a coupon for 35% for your next purchase, valid for 30 days. Your code will
  be available in your InformIT cart. (You will also find it in the Manage Codes
  section of your account page.)

Registration benefits vary by product. Benefits will be listed on your account page
under Registered Products.

InformIT.com–The Trusted Technology Learning Source

InformIT is the online home of information technology brands at Pearson, the world's foremost
education company. At InformIT.com you can

- Shop our books, eBooks, software, and video training.
- Take advantage of our special offers and promotions (informit.com/promotions).
- Sign up for special offers and content newsletters (informit.com/newsletters).
- Read free articles and blogs by information technology experts.
- Access thousands of free chapters and video lessons.

Connect with InformIT–Visit informit.com/community
Learn about InformIT community events and programs.

informIT.com
the trusted technology learning source

Addison-Wesley • Cisco Press • IBM Press • Microsoft Press • Pearson IT Certification • Prentice Hall • Que • Sams • VMware Press

ALWAYS LEARNING   PEARSON